PROHIBITION

~ IN ~

HAMTRAMCK

GANGSTERS, GUNFIGHTS & GETAWAYS

GREG KOWALSKI

AMERICAN PALATE

Published by American Palate
A Division of The History Press
Charleston, SC 29403
www.historypress.net

All photos in this book came from the archives of the Hamtramck Historical Museum unless otherwise noted. Cover photo courtesy of the Burton Historical Collection, Detroit Public Library.

First published 2015

Manufactured in the United States

ISBN 978.1.46711.753.1

Library of Congress Control Number: 2015946489

Notice: The information in this book is true and complete to the best of our knowledge. It is offered without guarantee on the part of the author or The History Press. The author and The History Press disclaim all liability in connection with the use of this book.

This book is dedicated to the memory of my mother and father, Martha and Joseph Kowalski, and to all the people of Hamtramck.

CONTENTS

INTRODUCTION

How could Hamtramck, Michigan, become such a hotbed of lawlessness and a national poster child for flaunting Prohibition?

Certainly there were some remarkable facts about the town. In the space of a decade, it went from a small farming village to a major industrial center. In fact, it was one of the fastest-growing towns in America, prompting a special census to be taken in 1915 that showed Hamtramck was growing at a rate fifty times greater than the rest of the country. The phenomenal growth turned Hamtramck into a cauldron of unrest as it wrestled with a host of social and economic problems brought about by the dramatic change. And it wasn't just a case of sheer numbers overwhelming the town. The community was going through a jolting cultural shift as tens of thousands of Polish immigrants flooded into the town to find work in the factories that were transforming it. Animosity toward immigrants is not a new phenomenon, and it was in full evidence in the early part of the twentieth century when Hamtramck was experiencing its wrenching transformation. The newly arriving Poles squared off against the German settlers who had come a century earlier, sparking a confrontation that produced an undercurrent of discontent and hostility.

By the mid-teen years of the twentieth century, Hamtramck was roiling in conflict that touched all aspects of its society. The 2.1-square-mile village of Hamtramck was wholly inadequate to meet the demands being suddenly placed upon it. Few streets were paved, and cheap housing was being thrown up at a furious rate by developers who acted more interested in pulling in a quick buck than creating a sound neighborhood. There weren't even any parks or green spaces for the kids to play in. The streets had to do. Juvenile delinquency ran rampant, and many of the adults showed behavior that was no better. Social services? Forget it. The concept was as foreign as the newly arriving residents.

The political scene was in shambles. The original German settlers who ran the village quickly became besieged by the Poles who wanted to make changes in the way the town operated. The landscape was already poisoned by the traditional animosity the Poles and Germans shared in the "Old Country" and brought over to America. The situation was chaotic and so challenging that no one seemed to know how to address it. Few even tried.

Then came Prohibition.

Utter nonsense would be a mild term used to describe Prohibition and its lofty goal of reforming America. It made even less sense to the immigrants who came from a land where alcohol was ingrained into society. For heaven's sake, the most sacred part of the most sacred religious ceremony for most Poles is the consecration of wine into the blood of Christ in Holy Mass. If Jesus has given his blessing to drinking alcohol, how could the government forbid it?

Even the purveyors of Prohibition knew better than to touch sacramental wine when they outlawed alcohol, but that did not placate the imbibers who saw beer, vodka, whiskey and brandy as sacred in their own way. They were not going to stop drinking because of some misguided law.

So on top of all their other woes, Hamtramck immigrants entered still another new world—one where the rule of law clashed with traditional values. It was against the law for the most part to make alcohol, to drink it and to sell it. But that was not going to stop anybody from doing exactly that. In fact, Prohibition drew a range of people into the mists of alcohol who ordinarily would never have touched the stuff. Kids routinely were drafted by owners of bathroom gin stills to haul hooch in buckets through the neighborhoods to waiting buyers. Infants were exploited as their baby buggies were outfitted with false bottoms and even their diapered bottoms were pressed into service to conceal liquor bottles. Ordinarily upstanding political leaders and businesspeople who never had run afoul of the law were drawn into the world of bootlegging. For some, it was a matter of principle. They felt the government had gone too far in dictating this aspect of morality. Others couldn't resist the fortune-making opportunities bootlegging offered. No matter how poor the local population was, somehow they managed to find the money to buy a drink.

And selling it to them was not seen as a moral failing. Breaking this law carried absolutely no stigma for a politician seeking office or reelection. In fact, sharing a drink with the constituency showed that you understood them and related to their needs and desires. And plenty of votes could be found in the illegal bars. Running a speakeasy did not necessarily make you a bad person. Leading businesspeople and highly respected community leaders ran illegal stills, speakeasies—and even worse.

Seemingly everyone got in on the act. Men, women, children and adults either made it, hauled it, sold it and/or drank it. The demand was bottomless, and the location for doing all of this was perfect.

Hamtramck is situated right inside the city of Detroit. Founded as a large township in 1798, it was swallowed up bit by bit by Detroit as that city grew. By 1901, a section of the township split off to form the village of Hamtramck, which itself incorporated as an independent city in 1922. What this meant is that Hamtramck existed (and still does) as an enclave, an island completely surrounded by the city of Detroit. But Hamtramck wasn't Detroit. It had its own police department and its own elected officials, all of whom could easily be handed a few dollars to look the other way when a Detroit politician, official or police officer wanted to slip into town for a quiet drink where nobody would bother him. Even other gangsters would see Hamtramck as a refuge where they could be left alone.

That's saying a lot. Consider that Detroit itself was a prime player in Prohibition. The city was perfectly situated on the shore of the Detroit River, just a mile or so from Canada, where liquor was far more plentiful. During the winter, convoys of cars loaded with booze made the quick dash from Windsor across the frozen Detroit River. In summer, bootleggers operated fleets of speed boats that could race across the river in a matter of minutes. And there were plenty of docks—some hidden inside shore-side houses—waiting for the boats. But in a way, Detroit may have been a victim of its own success. Its proximity to Canada and its thirsty population made it a lucrative link in the vast chain of speakeasies, brothels and gambling dens that stretched across the country. Heavy-duty gangsters, like the notorious Purple Gang, controlled operations in Detroit. Small-time players operated at their own risk.

Hamtramck was a different story. No one person or group controlled everything, but there was action enough for everyone. It was a welcoming place for the factory worker who just wanted to unwind with a glass of beer or a mobster who dealt with kegs.

All these factors converged in Hamtramck, making it a wicked witch's cauldron of trouble spiced with alcohol. The results ranged from humorous to horrific as the population was pulled into a vortex of crime, corruption and poverty even as the majority of law-abiding residents laid the foundation for a fine city in which to raise a family.

But that seemingly has been Hamtramck's way for more than a century. Contradictions abounded as the God-fearing Hamtramckans cheerfully tossed the rule of law out the window with a hearty *Na Zdrowie* ("Cheers," sort of). Yet they somehow managed to make a viable community that remains strong to this day. It's a tangled tale that even amazed the people who lived it and left outsiders watching the city in a perverse sort of awe.

Hamtramck was the Wild West right in front of them.

CHAPTER I

TO THE "STAMMGASTS!"

I t was all about power.

It was as simple as that. Forget about prestige. Forget about booze—at least for now—and understand that what made the system work, what drove people to do what they did was the seductive embrace of power.

That's what mattered. It made all the risks worthwhile and took the edge off the nasty things you might have to do to get that power and keep it.

The mood at Munchinger's saloon was grim. It had been like that for a while, and there was no sign that it was going to get any better. In fact, every day was a reason to feel worse. Sure, the town was growing, but with what? Those lousy Poles were climbing all over the place like bugs. This had been a nice, quiet town. Farms, mostly. A few stores on one main street. And, of course, the saloons. Like Munchinger's. That was the center of power in the village of Hamtramck as the nineteenth century flipped over to the twentieth. And it worked. No one outside the dusty farming town gave it much notice, so the five main saloonkeepers in town also served as the five village trustees and had things neatly tied up under their control.

To the "stammgasts," this was the best of worlds, literally. The stammgasts were the drinkers, the guys who propped up the bar at Munchinger's. They originally came from Germany, where they had spent centuries building up an

"Stammgasts," or German bar patrons, gather at A. Buhr's saloon in the village of Hamtramck in about 1900.

animosity toward the Poles. The feeling was mutual. Poland had been carved up repeatedly by the Germans, Austrians, Prussians and Russians, leading to the suppression of Polish government, education, language and culture. By the time Poland was re-created as a nation following World War I, the seeds of bitterness had long before taken root and flowered in Europe and America.

In America, it was a bit different. Here, the German and Polish immigrants declared an uneasy truce. Ironically, they often settled near each other, even sharing the same churches, at least until the Poles could split off and build their own churches. They knew what to expect from each other. But now the situation was getting out of control.

What happened?

Well, sit back and have a drink because this is a long tale. Don't worry, you won't be bored with a lot of needless details going back to the beginning of recorded time, but like any good crime story, you have to know who is who and who did what to whom and why.

It started innocently enough in 1798 when the township of Hamtramck was created out of the wilderness next to Detroit. The place was named for a French-Canadian, of all things, who made his reputation fighting for the Americans in the Revolutionary War. Jean Francois Hamtramck was born in Montreal in 1756 and came to fight for the Americans when they rose up against their British forefathers. Hamtramck legally changed his name to John Francis, and after the Revolution, he stuck with the young American army. He had seen what the British had done to his homeland in the French and Indian War and had no love for things English. Long after the Revolution was over, the British stayed on the "western frontier," which included Detroit, where they harassed the Americans and made a general nuisance of themselves. In 1794, when the new president, George Washington, heard rumors that the British were going to stir up trouble in Detroit, maybe even another rebellion, he sent Colonel John Francis Hamtramck to the Motor City long before its industrial engine started in order to kick the British out.

He did.

Colonel Hamtramck's troops took over the fort at Detroit in July 1796, sending the British splashing across the Detroit River and over into Canada. Colonel Hamtramck settled in town, and in gratitude for what he had done, the first Hamtramck Township, named in his honor, was laid out in 1798. It ran from the Detroit River straight up Woodward Avenue for about eight miles until it hit Base Line, which would later become Eight Mile Road. That line ran east to Lake Saint Clair. The township encompassed a huge area, although there wasn't much there except swamps and bears (including one that ate a kid some years later).

Most of the action in town—what there was of it—was clustered along the Detroit River. "Ribbon farms" were common. These were narrow plots of land that were only a few hundred feet wide but as much as a couple miles deep. This arrangement allowed more farmers to have access to the river while keeping the farmhouses relatively close in case of Indian attacks. Colonel Hamtramck lived in a log cabin alongside the river until he died, prematurely, at age forty-eight, in 1803.

Hamtramck Township was re-formed in 1918 and again in 1927, but that hardly seemed to matter. What did count is that Detroit burned to the ground in 1805 and then rose up in a growth spurt. Literally rising from its ashes (as its motto proclaims) it spent much of the nineteenth century gobbling up Hamtramck Township, which adjoined the city, bit by bit.

The swamps were drained, the Indians were pushed aside and the bears were slaughtered, especially after they ate that kid in 1857. Railroad lines— and this is especially important—began to cross the countryside. In chunks, the wilderness was urbanized. In 1901, a group of about five hundred Hamtramckans living near the junction of the Grand Trunk and Michigan Central Railroads about five miles north of the river took note of the ever-expanding borders of Detroit that were shifting their way and mapped out what would become the village of Hamtramck. Their goal was to preserve Hamtramck's identity as a town separate from Detroit, even as the big city crept up on it. Meeting in Holbrook School (which, incredibly, is still in use), the Hamtramckans marked out an area of nearly 2.1 square miles and went through the legal motions of creating the village, which the state approved, officially establishing the village of Hamtramck in April 1901.

The first village trustees met on August 29, 1901, in a house on the southwest corner of Denton Street and Jos. Campau Avenue. They were William Hawkins, Ernest Oehmke, Henry Mueller, Joseph Segrist, John Berres and Martin Wojcinske. Most of them were Germans. In fact, most residents of the town at this time were Germans or of German descent. The Polish community remained clustered about two miles south, in the old Detroit Poletown neighborhood centered on St. Aubin and Canfield Streets, where St. Albertus Church was built between 1883 and 1885. That was a raucous community in itself and in a way foreshadowed what was to come in Hamtramck, although on a minute scale. Despite the distance between the communities, there was a direct connection, physically and spiritually.

The drama of Old Poletown fills its own history books as parishioners and priests quarreled among themselves and with the archdiocese, which happened to be controlled by Germans. The disruption in Poletown, mainly over money and ownership of the parish buildings, eventually led to a riot that resulted in the shooting death of one man. In desperation, a group of St. Albertus parishioners loyal to pastor Dominic Kolasinski split from the parish and founded Sweetest Heart of Mary Church built just a few blocks west of St. Albertus. Although the situation reached an absurdly violent level, sanity eventually prevailed. By the late 1890s, tempers had cooled, everybody made nice and the community went about its business of growing.

In 1898, the Archdiocese of Detroit established another Polish parish—St. Stanislaus—several blocks north of St. Albertus, pushing the limits of Poletown farther north. By then the trend was clear: the Polish community was moving northward, and the numbers were impressive enough—some fifty thousand Poles were living in Detroit at this time—that the archdiocese concluded another parish was needed, one that would get ahead of the curve, so to speak, and allow the community to grow into it.

St. Florian Parish, founded in 1907, would become a dominating force in the community, nurturing the spiritual needs of the flood of Polish Catholic immigrants.

In 1907, the archdiocese scoped out Hamtramck village. By then, Poles were already beginning to settle there but not in large numbers. A survey of the community showed there was an interest in establishing a Polish parish in town. Accordingly, St. Florian Parish was formed and Father Bernard Zmijewski was named the pastor. The first Masses were celebrated in a store along Jos. Campau Avenue, the main street that ran through town. Soon a new parishioner donated a piece of land along the Holbrook ditch to the parish, and in July 1908, the cornerstone for the new church was laid at the intersection of what would become Brombach and Florian Streets. The new church was a combination building with one floor occupied by an elementary school and the other by the church itself. This was a typical arrangement for many new parishes at the time. It didn't provide a lot of room, but it adequately served the Polish community in the area. In short, it was good enough for 1908 but was going to become obsolete shortly after it opened.

Let's pause at 1910, for this was a critical juncture for the village. Take a look around. There's really not that much to see. At that time, Hamtramck was a dusty little village. Almost all the businesses were clustered along Jos. Campau south of Holbrook Avenue, which by this time was no longer a creek, having been filled in and paved over to provide the foundation for a road. Jos. Campau north of Holbrook was mainly farmland, although there were houses scattered across the area.

There were a goodly number of saloons, including the aforementioned Munchinger's. But sharing the landscape also were Cooper's, Buhr's, J.P. Kaiser's, A.P. Schroeder's, M. Kulczynski's, J.C. Adams's, L. Becker's and F. Bohn's saloons. There were a few grocery stores as well, plus a hardware store, the justice of the peace's office and some miscellaneous businesses. One of the most prominent buildings was the old Dolland farmhouse, which stood on the southwest corner of Jos. Campau and Holbrook Avenues. The German settlers called it the *kaffeemuehle* (coffee grinder) because of its unusual shape. It was considered somewhat of a landmark.

By this time, industry had begun arriving as well, prompted by the two rail lines that crossed town. Near one of them, William L. Davis and Thomas Neil opened the Acme White Lead Paint Co. in 1893 on the south end of town, and it quickly grew into a major operation.

Other factories began to spring up, especially after 1910, when Henry Ford opened his huge assembly plant in Highland Park, just about a mile away from Hamtramck. That also drew new residents to town as they sought jobs in the factories.

By 1910, Hamtramck had about 3,500 residents, still mainly Germans. And the beer was plentiful.

That fateful year, two men arrived in the village. They were interested in acquiring some property, and they took note of the area, especially at the south end of the village. There was a great deal of open space, it was outside Detroit where they might get a better deal on taxes and, critically, the two rail lines that crossed the track ran right up to Henry Ford's Highland Park plant.

That was especially important to John and Horace Dodge because they worked for Ford, supplying him with parts for his autos. The Dodge brothers were already well known as superb engineers who produced quality products. But they had bigger plans. They wanted to make their own cars. They already had a factory in Detroit, but it was too small and too confined for their needs. They wanted room to grow.

The Hamtramck site looked perfect. They quickly concluded a deal to buy a plot of land in the village and took possession in June 1910. They wasted no time in hiring noted architect Albert Kahn to draw up plans

The importance of the Dodge Main factory in Hamtramck's history cannot be overstated. It built modern Hamtramck. Without it, Hamtramck likely would have been absorbed by Detroit.

for the site. By December, they had the beginnings of their plant up and running and were building parts for Ford's cars there.

It would be another four years before they would be able to produce their own cars, but the die was cast, literally. They were the Dodge brothers—and note that it was the "Dodge BROTHERS." Send a letter to John Dodge or Horace Dodge separately and it would be returned unopened. They were an inseparable team who shared a determination to become great auto makers.

Never mind that they were also the brawling, hard-drinking, party-down Dodge brothers who were known for their barroom exploits. More than once they figured in newspaper stories recounting their latest fight in some bar in town. Although they lived in tony Grosse Pointe, just outside Detroit, they were shunned by local society. They had plenty of money, especially after they split from Ford, sued him for unpaid back dividends and got $19 million. They were well-respected businessmen, but as pillars of society, they were a bust. Eventually, they bought their way into high society through massive charitable contributions, mainly to support the Detroit Symphony Orchestra, but they never mended their ways.

Maybe they would have found the light if they had had a chance, but both died in 1920, John at age fifty-five and Horace at age fifty-two. Both died of pneumonia. Or maybe it was the Spanish flu that was sweeping across the world. Or maybe it had something to do with a lifelong infusion of alcohol. At any rate, accounts vary. But there was no question that they knew how to build cars—and sell them. In 1915, their first full year of production, they were already the third most successful auto manufacturer in the country, selling some forty-five thousand cars. And that was just the beginning.

It was a beginning for Hamtramck, too. Suddenly—and the word "suddenly" is quite appropriate—Hamtramck was launched into a period of growth that was unmatched in the nation. In 1910, there were 3,500 people living in the confines of the village's 2.1 square miles. In 1920, that had grown to 48,000 people. The increase was so great it attracted national attention. This item from the *Arizona Sentinel* newspaper of July 15, 1915, was typical:

> *Special Census of Hamtramck, Michigan:*
> *A special census of the village of Hamtramck, Michigan, made at local request and expense, shows the population of that village in June 25, 1915, to have been 21,520. The increase since 1910, when the population was 3,559, has been 504 percent. The present population comprises 21,242 whites and 278 Negroes. The census was taken by local enumerators under the supervision of an official of the Bureau of the Census, Eugene F. Hartley.*
>
> *Hamtramck is a suburb of Detroit, lying just to the northeast of that city. Its remarkable growth is due in great measure to the presence of large automobile factories within and near its borders.*

Dodge Main was the key figure in that growth equation in Hamtramck.

The Dodge brothers meant business. Their factory was not a minor affair. It was destined to be a major manufacturing plant that would not only rival anything Henry Ford had done but would also stand among the biggest plants in the world. And to run it they needed workers. When word spread that the Dodge brothers were hiring, Hamtramck became the destination of thousands of people from across the country, and even the world. Adding to the attraction was that soon other factories sprang up in Hamtramck, so there was an even greater demand for workers. Neighboring Highland Park experienced a similar growth, although not to the extent of Hamtramck. And Detroit, Highland Park and Hamtramck formed an industrial triad, with Hamtramck hosting two dozen factories alone. In addition to the powerhouse of Dodge Main, major factories like Briggs Manufacturing, Russell Wheel and Foundry Co., Chevrolet Gear and Axle Co., Champion Porcelain Co., Truscon Laboratories and American Radiator Co., among others, were founded.

Immigrant families transformed Hamtramck from a small farming village to a major industrial town in the space of a decade.

But in the case of Hamtramck, almost all the new arrivals attracted to the factories were Polish immigrants. Some came straight from Poland. Others gravitated to Hamtramck from other parts of the country, especially the coal fields of Pennsylvania. Poles had no fear of hard labor, but many preferred the grit of the factories above ground to the suffocating closeness of the mines below.

They came by the thousands. Soon the farms were plowed under and streets were laid out. Lots measuring a mere thirty feet wide by ninety to

19

one hundred feet deep were platted for houses that were thrown up by developers at a furious pace. About 80 percent of Hamtramck's houses were built between 1915 and 1930, and they weren't much. Basically they were wooden boxes with electricity and cold running water. Heat? Throw some coal into the stove. Hot water? Put a pan on top of that stove. Toilet? See that building out back with the half-moon on the door?

Or if you were a single man, you might rent a "room." Boardinghouses opened, offering men a chance to rent a space that measured about eight by ten feet with a tiny sink in the corner and a closet big enough to hold about three suits of clothing—one for work, one for home and one for church.

Still, this was better than what many of the immigrants had experienced in the Old Country, especially the opportunity to own a piece of property. Poles had a tradition of highly valuing the ownership of land, something that was severely limited during the partitions when Poland was under domination of the Germans, Russians, Prussians and Austrians. Landownership was a symbol of prestige, and while a three-thousand-square-foot lot did not constitute an estate, it was a treasure to be prized. That's one reason Hamtramck in later years acquired the reputation of a town where the people swept the streets in front of their homes and the alleys behind. People took great pride in their property.

But at this point, the critical decade between 1910 and 1920, there wasn't time to be prideful. The village was a mess. Roads weren't paved, many of the old wooden sidewalks still were in use (where they had sidewalks at all) and grassy fields were becoming filled with brickworks, cinders, scraps and other industrial debris.

In 1901, there were 252 houses in Hamtramck. In 1914, there were 2,061 houses, and by 1920, the number had reached 5,730. Most of the houses weren't worth much, but Hamtramck's real estate valuation rose from $200,000 in 1901 to $39,907,380 by 1920.

Now let's turn our attention back to St. Florian.

All wasn't so well at the two-story combination church/school building. Founding pastor Father Bernard Zmijewski dealt with a host of problems over financing the new church and ended up being removed from his post after, ironically, facing his own troubles with alcohol. Contractors were threatening to sue the parish over nonpayments, and the archdiocese was sending stern letters to the parish to clear up its financial woes.

Still, it was making its way through its problems and moving toward solvency. But even as that was occurring, things were about to change dramatically. These new Polish immigrants coming into town were mostly Roman Catholic, and where would one expect Polish Roman Catholics to go for their spiritual needs? Just as the town exploded with newcomers, so did St. Florian. In short order, the church/school building was made obsolete. Plans were drawn up for a new church building, one on a far greater scale. A huge foundation was dug and converted to a below-ground church right next to the old structure, which had been turned entirely over to being a school. The school is an indication of the growth, as every inch of space from the basement to the attic was pressed into use for classrooms. They were needed; by 1923, the building held 2,500 students.

Over—or, rather, under—at the basement church, as it would later be called, it, too, suffered from a lack of space although it was an improvement from the old building. But so many parishioners flocked to its doors that St. Florian parish split, forming Our Lady Queen of Apostles Parish on the east side of the village in 1918. The relentless growth continued, and in 1920, St. Florian Parish split again to form St. Ladislaus Parish, eight blocks to the north. It, too, would have its own schools for education, especially religiously based education, which was highly valued by the immigrants.

Soon St. Florian would rise to prominence, yet its foundation was fragile. The majority of the parishioners were poor. Many could give no more than pennies to the weekly collection plate that was passed around at Mass. But the church was so important that many parishioners mortgaged their houses to help pay for the new church. Some physically worked on the much more impressive structure that was to come in the next decade.

They did this because the church was extremely important to them. They viewed the church differently than people do today—not in terms of the building itself but in the church as an institution. It was not just a place to go to for an hour every Sunday. It was a social institution, a cultural center in addition to being a place of worship. These people came from a land where the government, when it existed at all, was largely ineffective and in constant threat of being deposed by its neighbors. They could put little faith in the rule of men, but the church was a bedrock they could rely on no matter what. That's what drew so many to it with such passion. This would become even more relevant during the Great Depression, although that was years away.

The church served many purposes. It was a link to the past and to traditions of the homeland. It was a pair of sheltering arms in times of trouble. It was a parental figure that provided spiritual and moral direction. This was a period when that was especially needed.

This "teen decade," between 1910 and 1920, was a time of great turmoil as unfettered growth changed the landscape. And it did not only in the proliferation of houses but in all aspects of the town. With development occurring so fast, there was no time or attention given to what we would today consider routine urban planning. Despite huge open areas that first defined the village, seemingly no thought was given to creating any town parks as urbanization enveloped the open spaces. Consequently, the kids played in the streets and on what few remaining empty lots were available. Recreation was haphazard, with no formal organization. That helped contribute to juvenile delinquency, which became a major problem as the town grew.

The school system, like the rest of the town, was overwhelmed not only in numbers but also by the changing culture. The one-room schoolhouse on Holbrook Avenue built in the 1890s quickly was replaced by a three-story building, and Hamtramck made a rare foray in capturing Detroit territory by annexing Carpenter School at the far north end of town into its school system. But still the need outpaced the supply. In 1916,

Awash with immigrant children, the Hamtramck public schools were forced to find innovative new ways to teach the immigrant children, many of whom didn't even speak English.

Hamtramck High School opened, straddling Wyandotte and Hewitt Streets. It at least was state of the art for its time, something that was rare in the village. And it was a recognition that great positive changes were needed as well if the town was going to have any hope of providing a decent education for the thousands of children streaming into the village. But while the schools were improving, they increasingly were facing a major cultural problem: how to educate immigrant kids—kids who often didn't speak English, who had health problems, who may never have seen a dentist in their still short lives, who had mental problems or issues at home. Poverty breeds abuse, and there was plenty of poverty in Hamtramck.

People weren't the only thing that Hamtramck had in abundance. Alcohol flowed with amazing freedom and in ways that would be inconceivable today. Nobody knows for sure how many bars there were in Hamtramck at its peak, but an estimate of two hundred is conservative. There likely were more than three hundred. It's long been said that Hamtramck had more bars per capita than any city in America, but it's hard to back that up with actual numbers. Still, just counting the number of buildings that once were bars is a staggering task even today. Old city directories list a dizzying array, especially as many changed hands through the years, assuming different names as they were taken over by new owners.

But one we know of for sure is the venerable Munchinger's, where we began this chapter of our sordid story. And, as we said, on that evening in 1916, the crowd was sour. They were watching their community change in front of them, and they did not like what they saw. They were facing a dilemma. The change, of course, was being brought about by the immigrants coming into town. And the most important factors facilitating that change, although not by intent, were the Dodge Main factory and St. Florian Church.

Unlike Henry Ford, who specialized in screwy ideas on how to reshape the character of his workers, the Dodge brothers were only interested in making and selling cars. Ford tried to dictate standards of morality of his workers. The Dodge brothers didn't bother with such trifles. They even brought beer into the factory for the workers on steamy summer days.

The bar owners certainly didn't like the competition, but what could they do? There was no way to drive the Dodge brothers out of Hamtramck, especially since once they broke ground for the factory, they didn't stop digging and building. Virtually from the day construction began on the factory to when it closed in 1979, it was being expanded or

A holiday-themed ashtray from Munchinger's gives no indication of the saloon's status as the political center of the town.

altered. At its peak, it would cover five million square feet of floor space in thirty-five buildings clustered on about 135 acres of land. It would grow to employ forty-five thousand people by the World War II years. It had its own fire department and was a city unto itself. But the people who worked there mainly lived in homes in Hamtramck.

The other prong in the side of the German saloon owners who ran the town—St. Florian—provided the spiritual and social comfort and contact the immigrants desired. And remember, St. Florian was established as a Polish Catholic parish. By its size and the nature of its being, it, too, was insulated from the ire of the German stammgasts. St. Florian was only going to grow and become even more important to Hamtramck. It was inevitable.

By the late 1920s, parishioners at St. Florian had enough resources to build this magnificent church. It stood as a sharp counterpoint to the corruption fostered by Prohibition.

The stammgasts were in a hopeless but not a helpless position, for they did have one big card to play: power. They still ran the town, and they understood the American political system. Democracy was a new concept for many of the immigrants who didn't yet realize the power of the ballot box. Even until the 1920s, just before Hamtramck incorporated as a city, the Poles failed to fully exercise their power. Writing in *Pipps Weekly* on September 24, 1921, Helen E. Wendell noted, "It was somewhat of a shock to me to learn that out of a population of about 50,000, Hamtramck's voting strength is less than 6,000. The only remedy, of course, for this is the

Americanization and naturalization of the foreign people that comprise the bulk of Hamtramck's population."

Prophetic words, but there wasn't much support for that from those in power then. When it was proposed that the schools hire a teacher of Americanization, only one member of the school board—the sole Polish member—voted for it. The concept wouldn't be visited again until years later when Maurice Keyworth became superintendent of schools. We'll hear more of him later.

The Germans used some more dubious means to maintain control as well. It was common for them to close the polls unexpectedly at 4:00 p.m. on election day, before the workers got off the job and could go to vote. Voter suppression is not a new concept.

But change was inevitable. In 1901, Germans made up about 95 percent of the village's population. By 1921, they made up about 5 percent. Facing such an overwhelming force of newcomers, cracks began to appear in the old guard's lines of defense.

In 1915, word began to spread that the village officials were talking to Detroit about having the city annex Hamtramck. How this would have benefited them isn't clear, although they might have worked out some sort of deal to retain local control. When the Poles learned of this, they formed the American-Polish Political Club with the aim of organizing the Poles into a political force. One of their first acts was to appoint a representative to attend every village board meeting and report on happenings there. They also began publishing a weekly newspaper in Polish, the *Kurjer Hamtramicki*, edited by G.B. Kosmowski, a well-known community leader at the time.

In 1917, the American-Polish Political Club petitioned the village council to hire a Polish-speaking person in the clerk's office to help the non–English speaking residents. The request was denied. Even so, a proposal to allow Detroit to annex Hamtramck was defeated by the growing power of the Poles.

The Germans had one last card to play, and that was that the people came not only under the jurisdiction of the village but also under Hamtramck Township, which coexisted for a time. Technically, the village was a part of Hamtramck Township. Although the township had largely been swallowed up by the growing city of Detroit, pieces of it remained and would until about 1926, when the final area was annexed by Detroit. But having two governing bodies gave the Germans two opportunities to control the government as well as the taxes that were levied on the people. In fact, the crushing burden of the double taxation also prompted the residents to go for the big change and have Hamtramck incorporate as a city. The question was put to voters

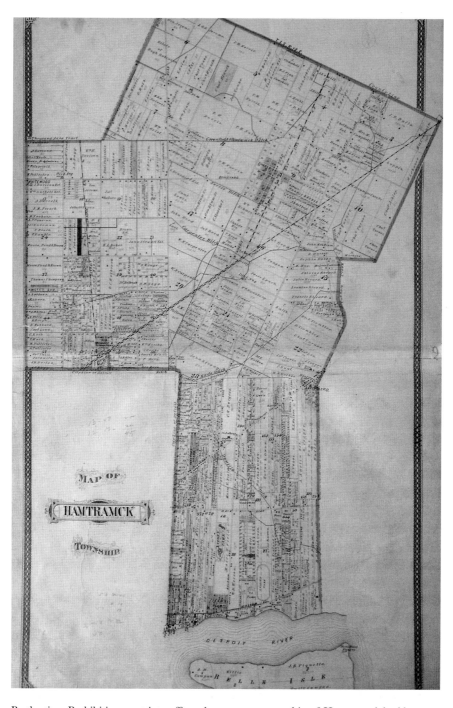

By the time Prohibition went into effect, the once vast township of Hamtramck had been almost entirely swallowed by the growing city of Detroit.

at the October 10, 1921 election. Out of the 1,100 ballots cast, 870 voted for incorporation. Accordingly, a charter commission was formed to draft an operational document for the new city. Of that ten-member body, at least seven were Poles. The finished document was sent to the state capital for approval, and on January 21, 1922, Governor Alex Groesbeck signed the document officially establishing the city of Hamtramck.

Tellingly, the draft of the city charter was published in the *Polish Daily Record*, as well as the *Hamtramck Times* newspaper. The first city primary election was held on March 1, 1922, and the first city general election was held on April 1, 1922. The results were mixed. Most of those elected were Poles, but the new common council included Dr. James L. Henderson, an African American. (African Americans, in fact, apparently played a key role in the formation of Hamtramck as a city by siding with the Poles to vote for incorporation. Without them, the measure might have failed.)

But the big winner was Peter Jezewski, a pharmacist who had been born in Poland and served as a state legislator in New York before coming to Hamtramck. He set the pattern for what was to come. From the long perspective, he led the Poles to political power, starting a steady stream of Poles and people of Polish descent being elected to office that would last for decades.

Peter C. Jezewski became Hamtramck's first mayor in 1922 and ushered in the era of predominantly Polish politicians.

But in the more immediate timeframe, Jezewski was elected in the early years of Prohibition. Temptation abounded, and he was poised to succumb to it.

By this point, the stammgasts were more miserable than ever. They finally had lost their grip on power. The German presence in Hamtramck would fade dramatically. And to make matters worse, they couldn't even get a drink—at least not legally.

But you can bet that there was no shortage of beer and spirits in Hamtramck.

Chapter 2

TO THE DRYS!

America had a drinking problem. It went back as far as America did—farther, really. In 1657, the General Court of Massachusetts banned the sale of alcoholic beverages. Farmers in Connecticut formed a temperance association in 1789, with folks in other states following suit through the years. In 1835, things got more serious when the American Temperance Society was founded and propelled by preachers. Liquor was demonized and seen as a corruptor of morality. The movement faded somewhat during the Civil War but picked up momentum with the creation of the national Prohibition Party in 1869 and the Woman's Christian Temperance Union in 1873.

Women, in fact, became the key players in the prohibition movement. That made sense. After all, they felt the wrath of drunken, abusive husbands. And in those days, there was little they could do to protect themselves. The system was tilted heavily in favor of men. Women couldn't even vote at that time.

But they weren't powerless. Some, like famed prohibitionist Carrie Nation and her ladies' support group, stormed into bars with hatchets and smashed liquor bottles. Although such incidents of violence were rare, the women often would sing, pray and urge saloonkeepers to not sell alcohol. While they couldn't yet vote, they did have authority. The women in the home often were the moral arbiters of the family, exercising a lot of control over the household.

Efforts also were made to reach out to the children, to steer them on a path away from the evils of drink by building a support base of non-drinkers to support prohibition. But boys will be boys, and liquor was cheap. And if you couldn't buy it, you could make it. And if mom or the missus didn't like you drinking it in the kitchen, there was always the barn or even the outhouse, which also offered a handy place to dispose of the empty bottles.

Politically, the country split into two camps: the "drys" supporting prohibition and the "wets" opposing it. This led to all kinds of political shenanigans in various cities and states as the two forces clashed and tried to elect their own kind to office. The drys had the edge, however; God was on their side. Numerous religious denominations from Quakers to Catholics (but not all) supported prohibition. About the best the wets could muster was the argument that the government shouldn't decide what was moral. The Anti-Saloon League, founded in 1893, may not have said that, but it sure promoted it, at least in regard to liquor. The league was founded as a state society in Oberlin, Ohio, but quickly became a national organization, superseding other prohibition groups, and was the leading force behind the adoption of the Eighteenth Amendment in 1920 instituting Prohibition—not the moral concept but Prohibition, the law of the land.

But in the late eighteenth and early nineteenth centuries, there is no indication that prohibition had any traction in Hamtramck. Until the village of Hamtramck was formed in 1901, Hamtramck was a township, one that was gradually disappearing as it was being systematically gobbled up by Detroit. Detroit had a long, troubled history with alcohol dating from its founding in 1701 by Antoine Laumet de La Mothe, sieur de Cadillac. He and the French fur traders introduced the concept of using liquor to trade with the Indians. Perhaps "trade" isn't the right word. In fact, they used alcohol to get the Indians drunk so they could swindle them out of the furs they brought in. Commandant Pierre Jacque Payan de Noyan, who was in charge of Fort Pontchartrain at Detroit from 1739 to 1742, to his credit, tied to stop this "shameful" practice and did shut down the flow of brandy that was so popular in Detroit—for a year. But there was too much money to be made in the fur trade, and ultimately the only thing he managed to achieve was to become the most unpopular man in town.

The practice continued, and in fact, the British used rum as a weapon, knowing it could destroy the Indian civilization. Chief Pontiac, the great Ottawa Indian leader in Detroit at the time, recognized that as well, noting that if his warriors settled by Detroit, they would always be drunk.

By 1774, even the British had had enough of the dangers posed by liquor and passed laws forbidding its sale to Indians and ordering that all liquor be stored in a "general rum store." That accomplished nothing. And it wasn't just Indians who were problem drinkers. Drinking was pandemic, as even children

Breweries were part of Hamtramck from its earliest days. The Peninsular Brewery stood by the Detroit River in Hamtramck Township.

commonly drank. Everyone drank and drank often. People had beer with breakfast and an assortment of drinks throughout the day, including cider, rum, wine, sherry, whiskey and even champagne. And if you couldn't get any of those, you could have "weed wine," which was made of nearly anything that would ferment. The idea was to get a healthy glow that could be maintained all day by steady but not overwhelming doses of alcohol.

There were many venues to sate that thirst. In 1834, when Detroit had a population of fewer than five thousand people, one hundred of them had licenses to sell liquor. Bars abounded, and they were often filled to overflowing with customers. In response, the city passed an ordinance prohibiting the sale of liquor in quantities of less than one gallon by any person unless licensed, and it fixed the license at fifty dollars.

In 1855, the state took things a step further with the passage of the Prohibitory Law, which ordained that no one could sell liquor except druggists, and they could do so only for medicinal, scientific, manufacturing or religious purposes. The law went into effect in May 1855, forcing the closing of all saloons. By June, they were all open again. Many persons were arrested for violating the law, but their cases were usually dismissed. So the law just faded away.

There were other outlets for liquor besides saloons. An unexpected source was pharmacies, which sold liquor for medicinal purposes, and indeed, in the days before the Food and Drug Administration, plenty of "medicines" themselves were no more than alcohol. Sure, you felt better when you took that "medicine"—at least for a while.

Grocery stores were another liquor outlet, with some grocers making their own and even having bars in their stores. Silas Farmer, in his landmark *History of Michigan and Detroit* published in 1884, noted that "the word grocery was synonymous with saloon." In fact, grocers became a target of early temperance groups in the city. The drys were there, holding rallies and prayer meetings and engaging in confrontational activities, like sending kids into saloons in search of wayward fathers and taking down the names of men who frequented the bars in an intimidating fashion. The Temperance Society of Detroit formed in February 1830 and remained active through the years. The drys remained true to their cause, continuing to push prohibition laws. In July 1858, 668 ladies signed a petition reciting the evil effects of liquor, which led to the closing of saloons at 11:00 p.m. It wasn't a big step, but it was progress in their eyes. In 1862, Detroit passed an ordinance to close saloons on Sundays, but no effort was made to enforce it. Following the Civil War, the issue arose again, and the Sunday closing was finally enforced in 1865.

Under the heading of "A Quiet Sunday," a Detroit newspaper noted on a Monday: "For the first time in years the great city of Detroit yesterday observed, outwardly at least, the first day of the week with becoming solemnity. All saloons, bars and beer gardens were closed."

The saloonkeepers were not pleased. In fact, they were furious. On September 1, 1865, they held a mass meeting at Campus Martius in downtown Detroit, and the next day, a petition signed by 8,265 Detroiters was presented to the city council asking that the Sunday closing law be repealed. A counter petition signed by 2,500 people in support of Sunday closing was also presented to the council. Three reports were drafted by the council, with the majority report calling for saloons to be open on Sunday afternoons until 10:00 p.m. But the mayor didn't like it, so the council reconsidered the matter and came up with a new series of regulations specifying hours of operations for saloons, as well as barbershops, groceries and even stables, which fared the best as they got to stay open as long as they wanted. Saloons were limited to 2:00 to 10:00 p.m. on Sundays if no games were allowed on the premises.

They stayed open all day anyway.

In 1869, a court ruled the city had no power to regulate what happened on the Sabbath. So around and around it went as the wets and drys danced a tango of conflicting philosophies. It's not surprising that saloons became the focal point of the struggle. Over time, bars had become more than places to drink. They turned into social centers, places where men would meet to talk politics, labor or some other issue. Early on, politicians recognized this and used bars as places to campaign and even as sources of power. This seemingly odd arrangement played out numerous times in Hamtramck's history and even continues to this day.

But at the turn of the nineteenth to the twentieth century, when women still couldn't vote, the saloons were important places for the men in charge. This was a time when Detroit's population was edging upward, reaching over 285,000 people by 1900. Then a new element was introduced into the brew: the burgeoning auto industry. Detroit was already recognized as an important center of streetcar and carriage production, and when capitalists who had made their fortunes in such areas as lumber and mining were looking for new ventures, they considered autos. They linked up with entrepreneurs like Ransom E. Olds and Henry Ford to build automobiles. Soon carriage factories were being converted to auto plants. After all, the earliest cars essentially were carriages with motors instead of horses. More than one thousand different auto makers would rise and fail as that vast pool would eventually dry up in the fiercely competitive and often cutthroat auto industry. But those who did succeed—like Henry Ford and, later, the Dodge brothers—did so in a mighty big way. They virtually transformed how much of the world moved, and they certainly mobilized America.

But they didn't do it alone. They needed help. A lot of it. And that introduces the second transformational element: the workers.

As the auto industry picked up momentum, so did sales. A relative handful of cars were built in 1900, but that number increased steadily every year until the United States entered World War I. Henry Ford built his first major factory, the Piquette plant in Detroit, in 1904, and by 1910, he had replaced it with a massive factory in Highland Park.

All across the metro Detroit area, including the villages of Hamtramck and Highland Park, auto plants were rising at a rapid rate. General Motors, Studebaker, Packard and others built some astonishingly huge factories, really factory complexes. The Dodge plant built beginning in 1910 in Hamtramck, for example, was actually a series of buildings including a power house, foundry, paint shops and even showrooms where cars could be bought. The assembly buildings alone were about one thousand feet long.

Even more factories arose to serve as suppliers to the auto industry. Detroit, Hamtramck and Highland Park all were growing at a furious

As the village grew to massive proportions, it faced big-city demands, leading to the acquisition of modern firefighting equipment and a vastly expanded police force.

rate. This increased the need for more workers. They came in a steady flow from across America and even Europe. Detroit had a long history of immigration. The French and later the British displaced the native Indian population. And throughout the nineteenth century, various immigrant groups settled in the city. The Irish came to the city in the early nineteenth century, followed by the Poles and Germans in mid-century and Greeks and Italians at the end of the nineteenth century and into the early years of the twentieth. But their numbers were small compared to what was to come with the auto boom, which also would attract African Americans as well as poor white folks from the South.

All of America was changing from a rural landscape to an industrial one. Society as a whole was evolving, but a fondness for alcohol remained as a constant among nearly everyone regardless of ethnic background. Those Poles who were transforming Hamtramck into their own town may not have cared to share a beer with the stammgasts at Munchinger's, but they sure would have taken the beer.

So in the teen years of the twentieth century, all these elements were flowing together in Hamtramck. There were the different, and often rival, ethnic groups sharing space. The change from being a rural village to an industrial town was occurring, and the wet and dry forces were at odds over drinks and drinking.

Prohibitionists may not have found much support in Hamtramck, at least at this point, but their forces were hard at work on a national level. And the immigrants fit right into the plans—in a sometimes ominous way. World War I sparked a rush of patriotism, which was adopted by the drys, who also capitalized on a distrust of immigrants. They were different. They

Communist Party of the U. S. A.
(Section of the Communist International)

Membership Book No. 10487

for

Name *Joe Meka*

Date Admitted to Communist Party. *1933*

Entered Revolutionary Movement... *1933*

District *7* ... City *Hamtramck*

Section ... *8* ... Shop or Street Nucleus

Signature of Member (in ink) *JOE MEKA*

This Book was issued on *Feb 20/33*
(date)

Signature of District Organizer and Party Seal

No Party Membership Book Valid Unless It Has Party Seal Stamped On

Issued by the Central Committee, C.P.U.S.A.

Many immigrants were perceived to be Communists by the people already living in this country. In fact, some were.

could not be trusted. Their loyalty was questionable. After the Russian revolution of 1917, many asked, "Are they Communists set on overthrowing our government?" It didn't matter if they didn't come from Russia. They all were lumped into the mass labeling as "foreigners."

The drys used this as political leverage, working their way into state legislatures and fostering prohibition. As early as the 1890s, some states had adopted laws giving counties and towns the option of voting to ban alcohol. Prohibition was in effect in nine states by 1913, and thirty-one other states allowed counties and towns to make up their own minds on the issue.

Step by step, state by state, the drys were gaining the advantage.

It came to a head in December 1917, when a constitutional amendment was passed by the U.S. House and Senate calling for national Prohibition.

The measure went to the states, and by January 1919, thirty-six of the then forty-eight states had ratified the measure.

Michigan, however, was already entangled in prohibition. It had started to go dry in 1918 when Michigan lawmakers passed a statewide prohibition. That was challenged in court, and the state supreme court ruled it unenforceable. Another prohibition law was passed in 1919, but before it could be challenged, it was superseded by passage of the Eighteenth Amendment instituting Prohibition nationwide. In October 1919, the Volstead Act was enacted, spelling out the banning of the manufacture, sale and transportation of intoxicating liquor while allowing it to be available for certain uses, such as manufacturing processes and religious ceremonies (medical purposes came later). But as for stepping down to the local bar for a quiet drink or picking up a bottle of wine at the liquor store, forget it.

At midnight on January 17, 1920, Prohibition went into effect.

America had gone dry.

But what did it mean? Was this the end of the stammgasts? Would Munchinger's and the other bars close their doors for good? Would all the people suddenly find the path to truth, justice, righteousness and sobriety?

Perhaps. Perhaps not.

Hamtramck gave a collective shrug. The immediate result was the closing of the bars and breweries, which would have impacted the local folks greatly. The stammgasts, who still had considerable political power at this point, retreated behind the now-closed doors of their bars and drank in private. While Prohibition outlawed the sale and manufacture of liquor, it did not forbid drinking it. So if you were a wealthy guy, you could have stockpiled up a basement full of bottles of your favorite spirits. But most of the people of Hamtramck were not wealthy. In fact, the majority were poor, barely eking out a living on the slavish wages paid by the factories. Sure, they could afford a bottle of beer, but the idea of having a wine cellar was preposterous. Still, they were not going to change their drinking habits. Alcohol had been part of their heritage and culture, and they weren't about to suddenly go dry.

It must have been enormously confusing for the newest immigrants. Not only did they come from countries where drinking was a part of life, but they also found America virtually awash in alcohol. It was even present in the workplace. The Dodge brothers shared a great fondness for strong drink and, as stated earlier, would haul barrels of beer into their factory on hot summer days. It wasn't exactly air conditioning, but it did keep the guys from walking out. What it did for quality control is not recorded, yet sales of Dodges only increased yearly. But suddenly confronted with Prohibition, the workers had to cope with the challenge of stark sobriety. It was a disturbing situation.

Still, they learned ways of dealing with that, as we will get to soon. But for some, Prohibition was life changing in ways they could not get around. Joseph and Stanislav Chronowski were two such persons. Born in Poland in the 1880s, they came to America in 1898 and in 1910 found themselves in the village of Hamtramck, where they organized the Auto City Brewing Company. Located on the south side of town, near the big Dodge plant, the name seemed most appropriate. It wasn't large, just a three-story brick building designed to produce some twenty-five thousand barrels of beer a year. But it was embraced by the locals, who pushed its sales up. Output nearly doubled by 1914, just as the Dodge brothers produced their first cars. The future appeared ensured until the curtain fell for the final act in 1918 when Michigan went dry. Auto City Brewing Company had to close. Or did it? Joseph went off on his own and founded Liberty State Bank, which became so successful that it was one of the few banks in Hamtramck that would survive the Great Depression. (Ironically, many of the buildings that housed banks that didn't survive the Depression later were turned into bars.) Stanislav and some other family members tried producing soft drinks at their former brewery for a few years, as was common among other closed breweries, but the plan fizzled. After that, the building was leased to another relative who simply reopened the brewery. Well, it's not that he put a bright sign on the front door announcing there was beer for sale, but he did start brewing the stuff again—at least until the feds found out, raided the place and tossed him in Leavenworth Prison. In 1928, Joseph and Stanislav returned to the brewery and began producing liquid malt, which was legal, and they later went back into the production of beer after Prohibition ended but failed to find the fire again as they battled increasing competition. The brewery closed in 1941.

Auto City wasn't the only brewery in Hamtramck. Casimir Kocat opened a plant to manufacture malt in Hamtramck in 1923. A decade later, when Prohibition ended, the plant turned to producing beer and found quick success. C&K Brewing Company was a hit, but Kocat wanted to retire. With its record of success, he sold the plant and left the state. Without his strong ties to the Polish community, which the new owners lacked, the brewery closed in 1936 and was sold at auction two years later.

C&K's story was not typical, however. Most breweries suffered great, even terminal, consequences when Prohibition went into effect. Some tried the Auto City route of selling soft drinks or producing malt, and others resorted to illegally manufacturing beer. But many simply closed for good.

Above: Auto City Brewery (at left) was one of the principal breweries in Hamtramck. It reopened after Prohibition but wasn't able to survive the competition.

Left: Shadows of the past: bottles and barrels from Auto City Brewery can be found even today, although they are rare.

C&K Brewery was successfully revived by owner Casimir Kocat after Prohibition. But after he sold it to new owners, they weren't able to keep it afloat.

What was clear, however, is that Prohibition added a new layer of chaos to an already overwhelmed community, and the timing could not have been worse.

When Prohibition went into effect in Michigan, relations between the German and Polish factions in town had reached the boiling point. Hamtramck physically was a massive mix of industry, commercial and residential properties seeming thrown together with no particular order. Jos. Campau Avenue was rapidly morphing into a major shopping district, becoming the new center of the community, and people were everywhere, literally living on top of one another as two-, three- and even four-family houses became the norm. The most common style house was the upper and lower flats for families to live upstairs and downstairs. In extreme cases, the house would be subdivided into two three-room flats on the first floor and two three-room flats above. Each three-room configuration might house a family of six or eight members. Hamtramck, in a sense, became one giant apartment building.

Village hall was built in 1914 at Jos. Campau Avenue and Grayling Street. In the depths of Prohibition, speakeasies operated nearly next door.

The growth was so rapid that the school system quickly became overwhelmed and went into a building boom in the 1920s to try to catch up and house the growing student population that went from 2,082 in 1916 to 7,657 by 1922. There wasn't even a proper village hall. A beautiful building had been erected in 1914 on Jos. Campau Avenue at Grayling Street that housed the village offices and police and fire station. But it was vastly undersized, so village offices were scattered across town. That made accountability more challenging, especially as developers were coming into town, buying property and erecting new buildings.

Cracks began to form in the system. Even in its last days as a village just as Prohibition was going into effect, Hamtramck was developing a reputation as a less-than-reputable town. The county prosecutor began looking into Hamtramck's affairs with increasing regularity as more reports of liquor, gambling, prostitution and associated crimes surfaced. Investigations were held, grand juries were formed and court dockets were filled with Hamtramckans.

Writing in the *Dearborn Independent* newspaper in August 1921, reporter Henry L. Commons noted:

> *Despite frequent grand jury investigations and reform campaigns, it seems impossible to do much for the civic conscience of Hamtramck. Just about the time the governor and prosecuting attorney think they have things going smoothly in this town, some assessor will forget to put a $1,000,000 corporation on the assessment rolls; some public building will cave in or some member of the police force will get locked up for highway robbery. Some of the public funds disappear in a manner which can scarcely be credited to so comparatively innocent a cause as inefficiency.*

Commons then went on to recount a story of a reporter who went to Hamtramck to do a story on Prohibition enforcement and met with the chief of police:

> *"I know where we can get a good glass of real beer," said the chief to the scribe. They were already on their way.*
>
> *"I don't want any of my men to see us," explained the chief, as they turned down a side street.*
>
> *They reached the railroad tracks and dodged switch engines and climbed into cars. They lowered themselves through a coal chute, ruining clothes and complexions. When they landed in the engine room of the brewery they*

were dirty and thirsty but satisfied that they had escaped prying eyes. They climbed a stairway and entered the tap room. They were greeted with lusty cheers from seven men who had long preceded them.

Just greeting from seven men who had lingered long in the tap room. They were seven of the most loyal of the chief's friends.

An imbibing police chief and officials with sticky fingers were just a hint of the problems. All the social ills of a fast-growing poor population were there, including crime. This news item from December 30, 1916, while shocking, became frightfully familiar:

"Little Girl Shields Baby as Robbers Kill Parents"

Detroit, Mich., Dec. 30—Meager descriptions given by Lucy Martyniak, five years old, who stood shielding her baby brother while three robbers shot her father and grandfather to death and probably fatally wounded her mother, furnish the only clues by which chief Barney Whalen and members of the Hamtramck police department are trying to track slayers of Joseph Martyniak and Joseph Jaskolski.

The two men were killed last night in their grocery and meat store in Hamtramck. Martyniak's wife, Agnes, was shot in the side. At Samaritan Hospital today attending physicians declared they were doubtful that she would recover.

Good luck in catching the killers. At the time, Hamtramck had a police department of a handful of men. Still, that was a hefty increase over when the department had only one officer back in 1901. More police would be added—a lot more. But each day it seemed to get worse. These were no mere growing pains of a town but signs that something was seriously wrong. And it was going to get worse.

No sooner was Prohibition enacted than people began to look not only at ways of working around the law but also making a profit from it. The answer, of course, was obvious: make liquor and sell it. The market was already out there, and with Prohibition being so unpopular, the risk of being caught doing something wrong was vastly reduced, at least in Hamtramck. As reporter Commons noted in that same story in the *Dearborn Independent* quoted above, several bars operated on the same block as Hamtramck police headquarters. "The proprietor of one of them across the street from headquarters, shut down his electrically controlled orchestra (a form of player piano) for a time until he found the boys on the force missed the music

Right: Barney Whalen (front row, left) became police chief of the village of Hamtramck yet somehow managed not to notice the speakeasies and brothels that flourished in the town.

Below: A typical illegal still. Hundreds of these once could be found in basements, attics and bathrooms all over town.

'something awful.' Now he opens the door when customers put a nickel in the piano and free entertainment is afforded the police."

Another factor to consider was Hamtramck's location right inside Detroit. Hamtramck's numerous bars, many of which became "ice cream parlors" when Prohibition came along, offered tempting refuges to Detroiters, especially higher-profile people like politicians, businessmen and even police who didn't want to catch the attention of the general public. And why stop at bars? How about brothels and blind pigs? They went hand in hand and were clutching money too.

If anyone had the slightest questions of conscience, they were not voiced in any lasting document. What we do have is voluminous files of court records and newspaper clippings recounting how Hamtramck was degenerating into a wide-open wild town filled with illegal businesses that were given a nod and a wink by the police and politicians.

Those two factions opened the doors to widespread lawlessness. They were in the best positions to foster, shield and benefit from bootlegging, prostitution and gambling. Don't like the bootlegger next door? Call a cop. When the cop doesn't do anything, call his boss, the chief. And when he doesn't answer, call the guy who appointed him chief—the mayor. It was a different sort of protection racket where everybody in power was in a position to cover one another.

For the most part, it isn't easy to sort out who was involved with what. Some citizens, like Arthur Rooks, were above reproach. Rooks was a prominent figure in Hamtramck's early days as a city. He founded a sports league, was elected as a justice of the peace and by all accounts was an upstanding citizen, serving the city honorably for decades.

But what about his uncle, Patrick "Paddy" McGraw? He, too, was considered a fine citizen. After all, he co-founded the Hamtramck Goodfellows, an organization that still exists to raise money for the needy at Christmas. He was noted for his generosity and fondness for stray animals, which he took in and gave a warm home.

He was also known for running one of the biggest brothels in the Midwest. It also was a wide-open saloon that made no secret of its operations. Paddy took his cue from the auto industry and instituted an assembly line where the guys would come in and progress up the stairs in line to the waiting ladies. The system was so successful that his place, right on the railroad tracks on the south end of town, drew guys from as far as Toledo, Ohio, about sixty miles south of the city, and Port Huron, about sixty-five miles north of the city.

That's Patrick "Paddy" McGraw (front row, right) in costume for some kind of weird event. McGraw was highly venerated by the citizens of Hamtramck—and operated one of the biggest brothels in the Midwest.

"The pleasure seekers, all sure of a good time at Paddy's, ranged from silk-hatted downtown business to dirty-faced, overall laborers," the *Citizen* newspaper wrote in July 1936 after his death. "Old timers, who have watched Paddy's progress in Hamtramck with a sly smirk on their faces, still recall that a Saturday night at St. Aubin and Clay streets resembled the scene of the Democratic convention in Philadelphia," the paper continued. The *Citizen* labeled Paddy's place as the "most flourishing saloon business in Hamtramck," Prohibition notwithstanding.

In fact, Prohibition was his source of success. Once it ended, bars "began to grow up like mushrooms" around his place, and he called it quits. He retired to his home at St. Clair Flats, on the St. Clair River, where he died under cloudy circumstances. The papers said he suffered an injury while working on his house. But others said it was a fight with a fellow known as Sailor Jack that did him in. In any case, Paddy McGraw remains one of the most colorful figures in Hamtramck's history.

Paddy made his mark in Hamtramck mostly during and after Prohibition, but Hamtramck was well on the road to moral ruin before the nation went

Ordine Toliver was a renaissance man with many talents. He also served on the last village council in 1921, the first African American to hold office in Hamtramck.

dry. And here, indeed, is a good place to pause and take care of one bit of lingering business: namely, the stammgasts. I recounted in the previous chapter how the German saloonkeepers clung to power despite the influx of Poles. But it was a hopeless cause. The flood of new immigrants was washing them away. Bolstered by support from the small but active local African American population, the Poles succeeded in approving the measure to have the village incorporate as a city. And the first city election held shortly thereafter in 1922 delivered the town firmly into the hands of the Poles. It's significant to note that Ordine Toliver, a prominent African American man, served on the last village council and Dr. James L. Henderson, another prominent African American, served on the first city council. But that didn't last long. Starting with the election of 1924, virtually all persons elected to office in Hamtramck were of Polish descent. That situation would last until the 1990s.

So the stage was now set. Hamtramck had become a city. Peter Jezewski was elected the first mayor, and Prohibition was the law of the land. Speakeasies, blind pigs and brothels abounded. By some counts, there were up to twenty-five thousand speakeasies in Detroit. No one knows how many there were in Hamtramck, but the number surely was staggering. Hamtramck had officially become a den of sin and degradation.

And the fun had just begun.

CHAPTER 3

TO THE WETS!

Charest Street is three blocks east of Jos. Campau Avenue and runs north of Caniff Avenue, nearly in the center of Hamtramck. It's a fairly long block made up almost entirely of two-floor houses done in traditional National style. They are all on thirty-foot-wide lots about ninety feet deep, which is typical for most of the city. Halfway down the block, about six houses in a row were raided by the Michigan State Police during a four-month period between January and April 1923. And that was just a small sampling of what was going on across the city.

By that time, Hamtramck, which just had incorporated as a city the year before, had developed a reputation as a wide-open town where Prohibition was viewed as an opportunity to make money. And almost everybody did, including the police and the politicians. The situation had gotten so bad that Michigan State Police stepped in and took over control of local police operations. What they found was a staggering amount of corruption. The state police conducted some two hundred raids, seizing seventy stills. Two breweries were uncovered. Many thousands of gallons of liquor, beer and mash were discovered and destroyed. It seemed everybody was involved in the manufacture, sale and distribution of beer and hard liquor. It was sold blatantly in stores and "ice cream parlors." Cars would even pull up outside the Dodge Main factory and sell liquor on the street to employees.

See that woman pushing the baby buggy down the sidewalk? Check out the buggy and you are likely to find it has a false bottom concealing bottles of booze. Or watch for the little kid carrying a pail. It's full of beer made by his

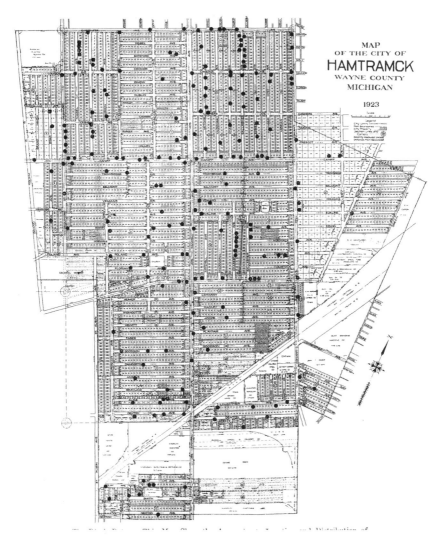

By 1923, Hamtramck was out of control, and the Michigan State Police came into town to take over law enforcement. This map shows the places they raided in a three-month period.

dad in the basement at home, and he's delivering it to someone on the block. Everybody saw it. Everyone knew what was going on, and no one cared. Well, almost no one. The state police certainly cared and did their best to put the bootleggers out of business and into jail. But even if you were caught, you stood a good chance of being hauled into court, where you would get off with a small fine—which just might end up in the judge's pocket. That's not to say that all citizens were satisfied with that situation, and some did fight back in certain ways. But the tide was against them. Soon about 150 brothels, including the especially notorious places run by Big Bertha Johnson and Paddy McGraw, were operating in the city on a 24/7 basis. Getting a drink was no more difficult than buying a ham sandwich—easier perhaps. Such brazenness did not go unnoticed. Hamtramck's corruption soon became a nearly weekly feature in the metropolitan daily newspapers—even in the Polish press. Editorial cartoons in the *Dziennik Polski* (*Polish Daily News*) depicted scenes of rampant corruption being ignored by the police and political leaders. *Follyology*, which billed itself as "A Digest of High Class Humor," carried an eye-opening feature on Hamtramck in its September 1924 issue. "The Story of Hamtramck Where Detroiters Get Their Booze and Night Life Thrills" delved into the seamy side of town with scathing ferocity:

> *On practically every corner and scattered in between are saloons—not of the near-beer variety but the kind where the finest vintages of Europe and the best of Walkerville and Cincinnati flows freely for a price that is only slightly above that of pre-Volsteadian times. Painted women, until recently walked the streets and openly flaunted their tainted charms from undraped windows. Gunmen lounged around lobbies of the city call and police headquarters. Both nodded greetings to the city officials when passing on the street. Cafés and restaurants, thrown up like mushrooms in the hurried scramble for a location in the oasis, blazed all night with a life that had long ago disappeared from these United States.*
>
> *Life was cheaper than liquor and blood flowed as freely. Guns barked in the hectic night and the police kept as well under cover as they possibly could... Vice and corruption not only went on under the noses of city officials but was participated in by them. And back of them, and their jobs was that powerful hand of the underworld...It is conservative to say that in every fourth house in Hamtramck there is either a still or a beer crock in operation.*

The article labeled Hamtramck as a "sordid city" where "graft, corruption and even bloodshed have cast their stigma." Some of it may have been exaggerated, but there was no denying the utensils of bootlegging the state police uncovered. By this time, Hamtramck's politics had become mired in a mixture of incompetence and corruption. It all came together as Prohibition was taking hold, and things had gotten so bad that by 1919,

George Haas was elected as village council president, running on what was to become a familiar platform of cleaning up Hamtramck's corruption. An architect by trade, Haas was described as "one of Detroit's most progressive and popular architects" by *Michigan Contractor and Builder* magazine. On Haas's election victory, the magazine noted, "he was enthusiastically supported and had the strong backing of the women voters. The liberal element, the People's Conservative Party, put up a strong opposing battle and it was feared that lawlessness would figure in the election."

The opposition was so strong that the state police were sent into town on election day to keep a calming watch over the polls. There had been rumors of violence aimed toward the women who had taken to the streets in support of Haas. But they were undaunted, and Haas prevailed, although by fewer than four hundred votes. "Now there will be a clean Hamtramck," his supporters said.

"He is already at work on his program of civic righteousness," the magazine noted. "He is determined to clear the village of vice conditions and the gambling practice." What he did do was rid the police department of police chief Barney Whalen. Chief Whalen was not implicated in graft, but he apparently had an amazing ability to not see certain things. Haas sought a replacement and turned to the Detroit Police Department for a recommendation. Fred Dibble had been with the Detroit police since 1901 and had been promoted to detective-lieutenant in 1918 before taking up the offer to come to Hamtramck in 1920. But the arrangement didn't work out well. Dibble and Haas had a disagreement, and Dibble was fired. And what a disagreement it was. According to stories commonly being circulated, the illegal saloonkeepers wanted to have a good working relationship with Dibble, so they told him there was a new Cadillac parked on Jos. Campau Avenue with the keys in it along with the bill of sale. All he needed to establish ownership at that time was to sign the bill of sale, and the car was his. Supposedly Haas learned of this transaction, raced to the car, signed the bill of sale and drove off before Dibble arrived. Dibble later confronted Haas outside Village Hall on Jos. Campau, and the two got into a terrific row. Bottom line: Dibble got fired.

But in true Hamtramck fashion, Dibble did not retire discreetly but instead joined the Victory Party, which opposed Haas's Liberty Party, and knocked Haas out of the box. Dibble and his whole slate—including John Kostanecki, Ovide Gravelle, Leo "Sunny" Hopper and Ordine Toliver—took over the village council. It was a short-lived victory, however, as Hamtramckans soon voted to become a city, and with that measure passed by the voters and approved by the state, a new election was necessary to name a mayor and common council.

Dibble jumped into the race. So did newcomer Peter Jezewski. Jezewski clobbered Dibble. Why? The answer is in the names: Jezewski. Dibble. Or rather, Polish. Not Polish. Dibble didn't stand a chance considering that Hamtramck was being thoroughly taken over by the Poles at that time. (As a side note, Dibble came back two years later to at least win a seat on the common council and bounced around politics in town for several years before Joseph Mitchell came along in 1930 to capture the city's non-Polish vote, pushing Dibble out. For six years, he remained unemployed before he had one last gasp in politics, winning a seat on the council in 1936. He died a year later. At the time, his total assets amounted to $5.35.)

After Fred Dibble was fired as police chief, he retaliated by entering politics—with mixed results. He died nearly penniless.

But back to Jezewski. Born in New York in 1883, Jezewski served as a New York assemblyman before coming to Hamtramck in 1917 to open a pharmacy. He settled into a comfortable two-story building at the corner of Jos. Campau Avenue and Belmont Street in the heart of the city's business district. The pharmacy became sort of a landmark and for years sported large glass hanging orbs filled with colored water. Inside the pharmacy could be found all manner of medical aids, including live leeches. But it was the room in the back, just off the alley, where the center of power rested. Here Jezewski met with the army of allies he built as they planned the Polish power play to take control of the town. Their strategy was simple and laid out before them. With all the crime and corruption overwhelming the town, Jezewski appealed to the voters with the familiar call that he would clean up the town.

Sure.

Perhaps there was a hint of things to come in Jezewski's inaugural address, which he delivered to the common council after thumping Dibble at the polls. He talked about recreation: "I respectfully recommend that you give immediate consideration toward providing adequate playgrounds for our children." He talked about welfare: "I urge upon you gentlemen that you treat generously the requests of [the city's new welfare department] so that we may say that the sun never sets on a hungry man, woman or child within the borders of Hamtramck." He talked about sanitation: "I pledge you my wholehearted co-operation in bringing to you the necessary improvements in our sanitation." But there was not a mention of corruption or any proposed methods to fight it. He did have a point in not addressing corruption in that at least he recognized that the city was going through some major changes as it developed at record speed. In his speech, Jezewski also mentioned the proposed municipal hospital, which was seen as vital for a major city. Although Hamtramck then had a population of about fifty thousand in 1922, the closest hospital was Henry Ford Hospital, founded in 1915 on East Grand Boulevard in Detroit, a couple miles to the west of Hamtramck. At the time, most Hamtramckans built cars, but they didn't own them, and taking the streetcar to the hospital was a daunting idea. Hamtramck Municipal Hospital would become a reality in 1927, but the city quickly learned that it did not know how to operate a big city hospital, and by 1931, it had leased the facility to the Sisters of St. Francis, who operated it as St. Francis Hospital until it closed in 1969. During its existence, thousands of Hamtramckans were born there and as many died there.

But death was not on anyone's mind in the wake of Jezewski's victory as mayor. Hamtramck was about as lively as a city could get, and Jezewski was well positioned to tap into that energy. As a Pole, he was extremely popular in town. His election delighted the local Polish population, who saw this as a major achievement nationwide. After all, Hamtramck was a large city population-wise, where much could be accomplished, as Jezewski outlined in his inaugural address. But politics intervened and soon reached epic proportions. While Jezewski had the loyalty of the masses, the council wasn't impressed, and supporters of Haas remained. Further, other figures were rising to prominence on the political scene, and Jezewski soon found himself in a political juggling act that seemed destined for disaster.

In September 1923, Councilmen John Buczko and Casimir Plagens introduced a resolution demanding that the police clean up the vice in the city or an appeal would be made to the governor to do the job. The council unanimously adopted the resolution without a word of discussion. Jezewski and Public Safety Commissioner Max Wosinski were present at the meeting but did not say anything either. Afterward, when confronted by the press,

Wosinski said he didn't see the need to respond to "every fool resolution offered by the council."

This resolution was prompted by the failure of a resolution passed by the council four weeks earlier demanding that a cleanup take place and making every police officer responsible for "conditions on his beat." To drive the point home, the resolution was placed in a gold frame and hung on a wall of the police station, where it was ignored.

The second resolution (not framed) gave a blistering assessment of the situation. It's fairly long but is worth recounting, as it sums up the seriousness of the state of affairs:

> *Whereas, the city council of the City of Hamtramck, upon the 21st day of August, 1923, passed a resolution making each and every member of the police department responsible for the conditions that existed on his beat in said city, and,*
>
> *Whereas, the reason for such resolution was the deplorable conditions that existed in the city of Hamtramck in regard to the number of disorderly houses that were permitted to run wide open due to the failure of the members of the police department and their superior officers to enforce the laws and the ordinances of the city of Hamtramck in regard to such matters, and,*
>
> *Whereas, four weeks have elapsed since the passage of the resolution and it is evident that there has been no further effort on the part of the police department or their superior offices to enforce the ordinances of the city of Hamtramck and to put these places which have been a disgrace to the name of this city out of business, and,*
>
> *Whereas, it would appear that these places must have some hold either upon the police department or upon those who have the appointment of the said police department which prevents the taking of proper action against them, and,*
>
> *Whereas, the proprietors of these houses have become so bold in their disregard of the laws of this state as to threaten decent and law-abiding neighbors with the destruction of their property in the event that they continue their complaint against them, and,*
>
> *Whereas, it is evident that the officials of the city of Hamtramck, in whom the power is vested by the charter and by the laws of the state of Michigan to enforce the law, tolerate these conditions to exist within the city, and,*
>
> *Whereas, it becomes a question in the mind of the council of the City of Hamtramck if such tolerance would not at least imply a reception of*

benefits from places which are not permitted in any other law-abiding community. Therefore,

Be it resolved, that this council deems it an absolute necessity that the ordinances of the city of Hamtramck and the laws of the state of Michigan be obeyed within the confines of Hamtramck, and that as officers vested with these duties by the charter have failed to perform as they ought and is required by the oath of office that they have taken when inaugurated as officials of the City of Hamtramck, the duties of their offices. Therefore,

Be it resolved. That this council demands of the mayor, commissioner of public safety of the City of Hamtramck, and members of the police department that they perform their duties as such and eliminate all disorderly houses from said city; that gambling be stopped; that places that have been denied licenses be put out of business at once; that transient merchants be stopped from selling their wares and merchandise in the public streets of Hamtramck without licenses; and that these officers be instructed to enforce all ordinances of the City of Hamtramck; that in the event of their failure to do so within the next two weeks, this council refer these matters to the governor of this state for such action in the premises as he may deem fit and proper in order that the City of Hamtramck may be made amenable to its ordinances and the laws of the state of Michigan.

Be it Further Resolved. That the commissioner of public safety of the City of Hamtramck be and he is hereby instructed to immediately file charges with the City of Hamtramck against all members of his department who have failed to perform their duty.

The measure is a mix of absurdity and desperation. No one could reasonably expect a police officer to be personally responsible for everything that happened on his beat, yet the corruption was so open and rampant that it was obvious the police were looking the other way. There's no record on how the police reacted, but there certainly was a legal response. Just two weeks later, a massive raid was conducted.

The *Detroit Free Press* reported on September 30, 1923, this item: "Hamtramck Dives Face Police Drive." The story read:

Raids on Hamtramck resorts last Friday night supplied sufficient evidence which will allow the prosecutor's office to institute abatement proceedings immediately to close nine disorderly houses on Clay Avenue, between Jos. Campau and the railroad tracks, Chief Assistant Prosecutor Robert M. Toms announced Saturday.

DODGE NEWS PHOTO

1929 DODGE PADDY WAGON -- Police had no two-way radio communication back in 1929 when this early model Dodge brought in the culprits. That year, commercial chassis represented about 20 percent of Dodge's output, a business which grew out of the firm's production of troop carriers, combat machines, screen-sided panel trucks and ambulances during World War I. The wagon shown here had a 140-inch wheelbase and a 208-cu.-in. engine rated at 63-horsepower.

While the police were largely ineffective in dealing with the rampant crime, it wasn't for a lack of equipment. This wagon was the latest in police equipment in the 1920s.

> *The sheriff's raids were instigated by the prosecuting attorney's office, he said.*
>
> *Evidence against five of the nine suspected establishments has been in the hands of Prosecutor Paul W. Voorheis for some time, it was said, but action was delayed so that abatement proceedings could be directed against all nine.*

What's really shocking is that Clay Avenue between "Jos. Campau and the railroad tracks" is a brief area that could be covered in a few minutes of walking. The places must have been virtually next to one another.

For its efforts in passing the resolution, the city council came under fire from the American-Polish Political Club of Hamtramck (Incorporated, no less), which threatened the common council with a recall and issued a petition of its own: "We are advising the city council for the last time to stop playing on our nerves; to stop degrading us in the eyes of our neighbors with resolutions of this kind, to give the city better protection through wise and proper ordinances."

The club went on to state that the council's action degraded property values and the statements it made weren't true. In fact, the council stated that conditions in Hamtramck were "far better than any city of its size in the whole United States of America and even the whole world."

Taking part in the public thrashing of the council was Stanley F. Jankowski, Hamtramck commissioner of public welfare, who wrote a letter to the council to accompany the Polish Club's resolution. He wrote:

Why blame the mayor for the conditions of your city? How can your mayor better a city without serious cooperation of your honorable body? Your honorable body has as much authority to do as much as Mayor Jezewski in this matter, so instead of sitting back and saying what ought to be done, why not become active and do yourselves that which should be done?

Personally, I think the city of Hamtramck is not as bad as your honorable body claims it to be. Would it not have been more sensible to get after things yourself instead of publishing in the headlines of newspapers such things as have been published? Why let Hamtramck glare in the headlines of newspapers all over the United States? The people in the city of Hamtramck have entrusted the name of their city in your hands when they elected you. Have you kept it as a sacred trust or have you put Hamtramck before other cities to be jeered at and ridiculed?

In reality, by all accounts Hamtramck was as bad as its growing reputation implied. But Jankowski had a point that the council was offering the city up for ridicule. Hamtramck was becoming the butt of jokes by vaudeville comedians as the city was becoming synonymous with vice and corruption. Yet it paled in comparison to Detroit, with thousands of speakeasies, where the Purple Gang ran unchecked and where corruption would reach to the highest levels, leading to the recall of Mayor Charles Bowles in 1930 on charges of protecting the rackets.

But Hamtramck made it easy for the press. If a reporter needed a juicy story, he could just go to a city council meeting, where he just might see a fistfight in the council chambers, or stroll down a street where the ladies of the evening plied their trade in the open light of day.

Jankowski had another point, however, one that deserved far more serious consideration. He wrote to the council:

Last June I set before you a proposition for the good of the people of the city of Hamtramck, that is, the Recreation Program. Immediately you selected two members and the school board also selected two more, then the matter was dropped—forever. Here is an example of the good work your honorable body has done for its people. Instead of starting at the root and building clean morals for your young people, the future generation, you do not give them recreation, but leave them to find recreation in saloons and places of vice. Why not take more interest and spend more time for these young folks?

The failure of the city in this vital service was shameful, and it was left up to the schools to fill that gap. (Which is covered in Chapter 4.)

Events, however, overtook the rhetoric and gave the newspapers something even more outrageous to write about. It reached a head in late 1923 and was recounted on the front page of the *Hamtramck Times*:

Hamtramck has witnessed many stormy scenes during the past score of years, but it probably can be safely stated that the past 72 hours have witnessed events of more far-reaching importance than any equal period of time in the history of this community.

Tuesday night—regular meeting of the council, at which the long-continued controversy between the council and Mayor P.C. Jezewski broke into flame, and a series of "near-battles" marked part of the session and a brief period of adjournment. A gun was drawn by one of the officials to protect himself, he alleged, after an assault and threats of more violence.

Adjourned meeting of council Wednesday afternoon, at which the council declared the office of mayor vacant and named Barney Whalen, recently deposed chief of police, to succeed Jezewski.

So what was this all about?

Well, Jezewski got really ticked off when he learned that some city workers were talking privately to John Buczko, the president of the council and the guy who later pulled a gun on Jezewski. It seems that when Jezewski heard about the hallway meetings, those who spoke to Buczko were fired, for various reasons. Buczko and the rest of the council were equally angry at Jezewski, saying that the council had every right to talk to any city employee and Jezewski had no right to fire anyone without good cause. Bringing things to a head, Councilman Paul Klebba introduced a resolution, which the council passed, firing employee Frank Stawski for not being an American citizen and demonstrating "Bolshevik proclivities." Jezewski vetoed that measure. The council overrode the veto. Jezewski, flanked by a cadre of "lieutenants," confronted Buczko at his desk in the council chambers to complain about the whole matter. Their discussion quickly degenerated, and at least according to Buczko, Jezewski struck him in the face. That's when Buczko pulled the gun. No shots were fired and no one was hurt, but a Hamtramck legend was born.

In retaliation, the council made Whalen mayor, or they thought they did. But why Whalen? If you can sort your way through this tangled tale that at times resembles a Russian novel, Chief Whalen was fired by village president George Hass and was replaced by Harry Wurmuskerken (we'll hear from him later). Whalen, however, remained politically active, and when Jezewski was elected, he named Whalen as chief again as political payback. But things are never easy in Hamtramck, and Whalen had his own political enemies, including Stephen Majewski, who was one of the two justices of the peace in Hamtramck. So to placate Majewski, Jezewski fired Whalen. That, in turn, infuriated Walter J. Phillips, the other justice of the peace, who happened to be Whalen's friend.

What did Phillips do? He went to the state. He, along with Wayne County prosecutor Paul Voorheis, brought the state police into town to take on the corruption, raiding speakeasies, bootleggers and brothels. It was during this period that Voorheis made the famous claim that Hamtramck was "the wide west of the middle west." Judge Arthur J. Tuttle went even further, calling Hamtramck "a disreputable community, a cancer spot and crying disgrace."

While the state police were in town, they learned of a midnight run being made by a convoy of liquor trucks coming into the city and being led by police lieutenant John Ferguson. The cops nailed Ferguson along with a host of others, some of whom spilled what they knew, drawing a line right to Jezewski, who, by the way, had worked his way around the council's appointment of Whalen and was mayor again. Or still was. Whatever.

There were indictments all around. Dozens of bootleggers, gangsters, politicians, police officers, blind pig operators, malt company officials and at least two ladies (however you wish to define that term) were indicted in federal court. There, one Mickey Squires turned state's evidence and spilled his guts. It wasn't a pretty sight. He described how he had been assigned a route to deliver beer locally by Lieutenant Ferguson. He said Ferguson bought the beer from a West Side brewery, upped the price and sold it to Squire for $20.00 a half barrel. Squire, in turn, sold the beer to the local saloons for $22.50 a half barrel.

"Ferguson took me around to all of the saloons, most of the time being in uniform, and we would take orders for the next day," Squires said. "Then he would call up Louis Silverman and tell him how much to let me have."

Police raids of home stills were common even long after Prohibition ended. Most were small operations, but some reached impressive proportions.

Silverman was the brewery contact. "Sometimes when Ferguson was unable to go with me I would go out and get the orders for the next day and call him up at police headquarters or go there and see him and tell him how much beer I wanted for the next day. I often paid him for the beer in police headquarters," Squires said.

Squires identified the saloons he delivered beer to and said they were under the protection of Ferguson. Adding to the jaw-dropping testimony was Albert Hamann, a driver for the brewery who said he had been hired for forty-five dollars a week to deliver beer to Hamtramck bars. He said he had been told that Hamtramck police would not bother him as he made his rounds. He and Squires both said they had a good working relationship with the cops and met them as they made their deliveries. Another witness who owned a saloon said it was a common practice not to charge police officers for a drink.

It got worse. Police officer Edward S. Redman testified that public safety director Max Wosinski warned him not to bother bars that serve "good beer and whiskey." Another officer testified he had seen Mayor Jezewski

Hamtramckans express their views in an anti-Prohibition parade in 1932. Their desire was fulfilled not long afterward. *Walter Reuther Library, Wayne State University.*

drinking on a number of occasions, including at a "beer festival" held in honor of Jezewski. Imagine—a "beer festival" being held in the midst of Prohibition in honor of the mayor.

Only in Hamtramck.

Still another officer testified that he had resigned from the force to open a saloon after the mayor barged into the police station one day, highly intoxicated, and ordered him to leave the bars alone. What may have been even more damning for the mayor was the testimony of another police officer who said he had seen the mayor and other city officials drinking at the Venice Café, which was owned by Chester LeMare, Hamtramck's king of crime.

LeMare was a product of New York's underworld, where he developed a bad reputation. Supposedly one morning as he was coming out onto the street, he was met by two detectives who escorted him to the police commissioner's office. There the commissioner informed him that he—LeMare—was leaving town, which was a surprise to LeMare. But he got the picture and was soon on his way to Chicago, where, coincidentally, he got the same treatment. One night he was on a train bound for Detroit, but by then he had wised up, and instead of walking into the arms of the police he knew would be waiting for him, he got off a few stops short of the Motor City. A few weeks later, he turned up in Hamtramck, where he opened the Venice Café. So this Italian opened a spaghetti house in Polish Hamtramck. It almost sounds like the opening line of a joke, but there was nothing amusing about Chester LeMare. He was a murderous thug who found the lawlessness of Hamtramck at the time suited to his lifestyle.

He quickly organized his own gang and operated speakeasies as he climbed up to the higher levels of metro Detroit's underworld. In 1930, LeMare ordered the murder of rival gang leader Gaspare Milazzo and his aide Sasa Parinno and proclaimed himself the leader of the Castellammarese Sicilian gangsters who were at the core of what became known as the Castellammarese War that broke out in February 1930. This was a New York–based feud, but LeMare had the backing of mob boss Joe Masseria, one of the principals in the war, who recognized LeMare as the leader of the Detroit underworld. The assassination of Milazzo and Parinno at the Vernor fish market by LeMare marked him for death, and he went underground after the killings. Barely a year after he became head of the Detroit mafia, he was tracked down hiding in a house in Detroit, where he was shot by rival gangsters on February 7, 1931. Police found a tear gas gun, six revolvers, two rifles, four thousand rounds of ammunition and several hand grenades in the house. None of them did him any good.

Although technically a businessman, LeMare hardly qualified as a candidate for the chamber of commerce. So Mayor Jezewski did not improve his standing in the community by being seen at his place. It certainly didn't impress the federal court jury, at least not in a positive way. Jezewski, Wosinski and Ferguson each drew a two-year sentence in Leavenworth Prison. A host

Stephen Majewski succeeded Peter Jezewski as mayor in 1927. But he accomplished virtually nothing as the city council members still were allied to Jezewski and blocked nearly everything Majewski wanted to do.

of others were also convicted, but if this did anything to clean up the town, the effects didn't last. In reality, the cleanup didn't even begin. In fact, Jezewski apparently viewed his conviction as a mere pothole along the road of life. Even as he appealed his conviction, he ran again for mayor, but he faced some solid opposition from one-time supporter Stephen Majewski.

Majewski knew Jezewski well and said he admired him. "We were all friends of the mayor," he said. But he also knew of Jezewski's shortcomings. Like Jezewski, Majewski came to Hamtramck from New York. Born in Poland, his parents brought him to America when he was a child, and he eventually got a law degree. In 1920, he came to Hamtramck and became acquainted with Jezewski and the Hamtramck political scene.

"Jezewski was a likeable man," Majewski said ten years after Jezewski was dead and forty years after Prohibition became nothing more than a bad memory. Majewski saw that Jezewski was the hub of the Polish community in town that the people had gravitated to, and he realized that Hamtramck was in transition, with the German old-timers mainly living on the south side of town, south of Holbrook Avenue, and the newcomer Poles living on the north side. The division was as deep as the old Holbrook Creek that once cut through the community at the bottom of a steep ravine.

Majewski noted Jezewski's success with the Poles and stepped into politics himself. He was elected justice of the peace for Hamtramck Township as well as serving as a township trustee and got to know Jezewski.

OK—just to be clear about this "township" versus "village" versus "city" stuff, let us review this: Hamtramck was founded as a township in 1798 and originally stretched from the Detroit River on the south to Woodward Avenue on the west to Eight Mile Road (known then as Base Line) to the north and all the way through the neighboring communities making up the Grosse Pointes on the east. The township was constituted again in 1818 and 1827. In 1901, the village of Hamtramck was carved out of the township, which had been periodically annexed in pieces by the rapidly growing city of Detroit. That 2.1-square-mile village incorporated as the city of Hamtramck in 1922, and for a time it existed concurrently with the remains of Hamtramck Township that abutted it. The last portion of the township was finally gobbled up by Detroit in the 1920s. And it was that last area of which Majewski became a trustee.

But it was as justice of the peace that Majewski held most sway. The courtroom is where he met the lawbreakers on a daily basis, many of whom were his neighbors. He, like them, had little use for Prohibition. "Prohibition was a really bad thing for this country. People who were otherwise law abiding citizens violated the law because they just didn't respect it. It made a lot of people violate the law," he said. His attitude was reflected in the courtroom. "If a man had a bottle of bootleg in his possession we didn't treat that as a felony," Majewski said. "You paid a fine." But he explained that if the person manufactured the stuff, then the feds would take over the case and the person would face some serious jail time.

It was justice, but it wasn't just. "I've seen cases where people in public office were absolutely drunk," he said. "They were violating the laws just as anybody who was furnishing the liquor."

Like many other people at the time, Majewski also felt that Hamtramck's reputation wasn't entirely deserved, or at least it should have not been considered any worse than Detroit. "Hamtramck was made the goat," he said. The newspapers sensationalized stories, he said. But that is the nature of newspapers. "They play things up that are of a particular interest to the citizenry." Still, there was no denying that there was an awful lot to play up, and not all of it was Prohibition related. Consider the fate of Warsaw Bakery on Jos. Campau Avenue. Early one morning in January 1922, residents in the area were thrown out of their beds when someone blew up the bakery. Owner David Rosen said it was rival bakers who objected to Warsaw Bakery selling bread at a reduced rate of five cents a loaf. Two people were slightly injured, and about $20,000 worth of property damage was done.

Jezewski had nothing to do with that incident, but he didn't help the sense of growing lawlessness. In fact, he set himself up as a target. Take his association with Chester LeMare. Jezewski used to like to eat spaghetti at LeMare's Venice Café. That was against the advice of Majewski. "I said to him, 'Peter, I wouldn't do that if I were you because it has a reputation and

Warsaw Bakery was on Jos. Campau Avenue, the city's main street. That didn't deter someone from blowing up the place during Prohibition.

you being a public servant, you can't afford to do that because suppose there is a raid by the federals and you're in there. There's an implication you are condoning certain things that are going on.'" And, indeed, he was.

"Jezewski was a good man, but he wasn't suited for the office of mayor," Majewski said. "He didn't have a firm grasp on the affairs of the city. He'd let things go." So did Max Wosinski, the police commissioner who ended up in prison with Jezewski. Yet in comparison to what police lieutenant Lou Hook did, Jezewski and Wosinski were pillars of wisdom. After imbibing, Hook decided to conduct a one-man raid of the Venice Café.

"He walked in and tried to arrest people," Majewski said. But LeMare's cronies were not impressed. They took his gun. They took his handcuffs. They took his blackjack. They beat him up. And to make matters even worse, they took the items they had confiscated from Lieutenant Hook to the police station and dropped them on the front desk for the officer in charge to see.

"To me, that was unheard of," Majewski said. But he didn't back down from the brazen affront. The men were arrested and charged with assaulting a police officer. "I gave them a $100 fine and 90 days in jail," Majewski said. After he sentenced the thugs, Wosinski asked him, "Aren't you afraid of the Italians?"

"I said, 'Max, you're the head of the police department and as such you ought to honor this man regardless if he was under the influence of liquor.' I said, 'I don't care what the circumstances were. He was a police officer and they had no right to do what they did. This was absolutely uncalled for.'"

While that episode was bizarre, it did nothing to change public opinion of Jezewski. But a far more serious event did. The Hamtramck State Bank was a regal, if small, Gothic building that stood nearly across the street from the old village hall on Jos. Campau Avenue at Grayling. That might seem to make it unattractive to robbers, but one day it was indeed robbed. A policeman responding was shot and killed. Even for those wild days, the murder of a policeman was shocking.

"That didn't set right with a lot of people who saw it as a general breakdown of law enforcement," Majewski said. With the population upset and Jezewski facing a jail term, there was a fear among the Poles that their newly won political dominance was in jeopardy. Majewski and other members of the Polish political machine met to weigh the situation. "A group of us got together," Majewski said. They formed Jezewski's inner circle, including Dr. T.T. Dysarz, who was a prominent politician in his own right; Walter Cytacki; and Frank Stafski, among others. They would congregate in the back room of Jezewski's pharmacy to discuss politics long into the night. Or they would meet in the garage behind Jezewski's Trowbridge Street house where Jezewski liked to tinker with his radios. Radios were just coming into vogue at the time and weren't very good, but Jezewski had a fondness for them. This was the group that propelled Jezewski into the political spotlight—and later sought to bring him down.

"We all liked Jezewski but politically he was in the wrong position," said Majewski. Wrong in the sense that should his appeal fail, he would go to

Hamtramck State Bank stood nearly across the street from the old village hall, which housed the police station. A robbery-murder committed there shook the community.

prison and council president Fred Dibble would automatically be named to fill the vacancy, as prescribed by the city charter. Dibble was from the German voting bloc, and none of the Poles wanted to see him as mayor. Plus, Majewski described him as a heavy drinker, which did not present a good image, especially during Prohibition, even in a town as forgiving as Hamtramck.

Several Poles were approached to run against Jezewski, but all refused. Finally, they turned to Majewski. "They insisted" he run, he said. "I never wanted to be mayor. I was forced into it." Even so, Majewski took to the campaign trail on the familiar platform of cleaning up the town. Running for office at that time could be grueling. Politics was played with a heavy hand. Dozens of rallies were held at the numerous halls in town where arguments were frequent and no one held back on attacking any candidate publicly. Take the case of Judge Walter Phillips who was running for office. He didn't speak Polish and was booed off the stage at a rally by members of the audience for delivering his address in English. The Detroit newspapers made much of this, even questioning the patriotism of the attackers. After all, wasn't English the language of America? Actually, it wasn't—or at least it wasn't the only language, as attested to by the millions of immigrants who spoke a host of languages. And the immigrants spoke loudly, especially at political rallies.

They didn't hold back their feelings after the vote either. If you lost an election, you might find your name prominently attached to a casket in a hearse that would be paraded up and down Jos. Campau Avenue. We often cringe at campaigning tactics today, but they are wimpy in comparison to the democracy in action in this period.

Majewski did speak Polish, and he defeated Jezewski in the 1926 election. Jezewski was carted off to Leavenworth anyway, although he wasn't about to give up political control. Majewski learned that quickly when he took over the reins as mayor. All the common council members still were loyal to Jezewski. "The whole council was against me," Majewski said. "Every one of them." They were still taking their orders from Jezewski in Leavenworth.

Although Majewski was a lawyer, his real devotion was engineering. Consequently, he wanted to be a builder of Hamtramck. He wanted to create a new recreation center. At this point, the city did not have a recreation department. What recreation was available was provided by the school district. He also wanted to build a viaduct, which actually did come about. That went in place on Jos. Campau not far from where Munchinger's saloon stood. It was desperately needed because of the railroad tracks just north of the Dodge Main factory. It wasn't unusual for workers rushing to the job to hop between the moving freight cars or even crawl under them as they blocked traffic on Jos. Campau. A number of workers were squashed in the process. The viaduct ended that when it opened amid much fanfare in 1927. But even that achievement was not done just with local support. Majewski had helped Governor Fred Green win the election, and Green repaid the favor with support for the viaduct. The viaduct was a major accomplishment, but in the big picture, it was a minor achievement. Another notable construction project was the opening of Hamtramck Municipal Hospital—later St. Francis Hospital—which occurred during his tenure. But that had been in the works for years, so he really couldn't take full credit for it.

While Majewski's intentions were good, his methods were questionable. It's not that he did anything improper; his strategy was faulty. To fund his projects, he proposed raising the taxes on Dodge Main. Not surprisingly, the folks over at Dodge didn't think highly of that idea and successfully fought it in court and at the state level.

So a common council that opposed everything he did and a faulty funding program constituted two strikes. A third was his rocky relationship with the police department. The police were highly political, at least somewhat corrupt and thoroughly in the pocket of Jezewski and his followers. And

Hamtramck Municipal Hospital was opened in 1927 to serve the growing immigrant population. It still has a pair of cells in the basement where drunks suffering from DTs were held.

by now the vice and corruption had solidified into the character of the community, and there seemed little that the state or courts could do or that the local police would do. Even sending Jezewski to prison changed nothing. He would still exercise a lot of political power from prison. So in essence, Majewski gave up. There was no hope of him stamping out corruption, so he just stopped trying. Rather, he just let the situation take its own course. If the feds wanted to come into town and conduct raids, so be it, although he was miffed at the amount of bad press the city was receiving, especially when such bad behavior in Detroit was given a pass by the newspapers. It must have been enormously frustrating, but it didn't stop him from seeking reelection in 1928. But the Jezewski supporters weren't going to let him get a free ride. They recruited a dashing—yes, he actually was quite dashing— young doctor named Rudolph Tenerowicz to run for mayor.

And so began one of the most colorful chapters in Hamtramck's history. Rudolph Tenerowicz, or Doc Ten, as he was commonly called, was born in Budapest, Austria-Hungary, in 1890 and came to America in 1892 as his family settled in Pennsylvania. For a time as a boy, he worked at a coal mine as a "breaker boy," who worked above ground separating slate from coal pieces. Tenerowicz attended parochial schools in Adrian, Pennsylvania; New York; and Orchard Lake, Michigan, before going to St. Ignatius College in Chicago, where he received a medical degree. After a stint in the army during World War I, he returned to Chicago and then moved in 1923 to Hamtramck, where he set up his practice. It was an event of at least some note as the *Hamtramck Times* carried his photo and notice on January 26, 1923, that he was establishing his practice at 9005 Jos. Campau Avenue, above Sidder's clothing store. Tenerowicz said he came to Hamtramck because he had heard it was a "promising city" of Polish Americans.

Dr. Rudolph Tenerowicz was one of Hamtramck's most popular mayors, so much so that a stint in prison did nothing to dampen his popularity.

There were two groups who had an edge in entering the world of politics in Hamtramck: saloonkeepers and doctors. Both had built-in publics that supported them and interacted with them on a regular and cordial basis. This was reflected in the number of mayors and other elected officials who were from both professions. In the case of Dr. Tenerowicz, he quickly developed a clientele of patients. In later years, he would build that by becoming chief of surgery at Hamtramck Municipal Hospital. He further strengthened his bond with people by often treating them for free when they couldn't afford to pay. Tenerowicz soon came to the attention of the political machine in the city, and he was quickly tapped as the candidate to run against Majewski by his political opponents. A quick call to Leavenworth sealed the arrangement, as Jezewski gave his blessing from behind bars to Tenerowicz's candidacy. Tenerowicz made quick work of Majewski, and after being in town barely five years, he was its leader. Essentially, what he got and what he gave was pretty much of the same. Bootlegging and corruption continued unabated, although he had announced that he would clean up the town and some people even swore that he had. One quoted person said he had restored Hamtramck to "almost pristine virtue."

He hadn't. But he was politically savvy enough by this point—despite making some rookie mistakes, like appointing former opponents to positions in his administration—to get a grasp on the job and build a powerful political base. He needed it. By the end of Tenerowicz's first term, Jezewski was out of jail and looking to regain his former political footing, although he preferred and backed venerable Dr. T.T. Dysarz to run for the office of mayor. But Jezewski and Dysarz had a falling out, and Tenerowicz breezed to an easy election win as the two friends-turned-rivals battled.

By now, Hamtramck's population was a staggering fifty-six thousand or so people all crammed in the city's 2.1-square-mile area. It had become one of the largest cities in Michigan, population-wise. But it was a mess physically, financially, spiritually and emotionally. There was barely enough room to hold all the residents. Families were crowded together, and city blocks were developed without much, if any, regard for what they would hold. Factories sat right next to houses. Small machine shops, stores, houses and schools—not to mention blind pigs and brothels—made for uncomfortable neighbors. In a way, Hamtramck should have been booming, and it was if you only measured the crowds and the buildings. But in a more important sense, it was staggering, and not just because of too much alcohol. Most of the residents who came into town were poor and of very modest means. The city had no income tax at that time, and property values were low, so taxes didn't generate enough revenue to support the burgeoning city payroll. Corruption played a hand in the finances in a number of different ways. A business owner could get a tax break by paying off the city assessor or might be left off the tax roll altogether. Cronyism also began to make inroads into the city as it became routine for politicians who were elected to give jobs to those who were important supporters. Jobs were created, like business scale inspectors and persons who could be described as park watchers. Just what their job was was debatable, but it didn't really matter because they weren't doing it anyway. They were working at Dodge Main while they were being paid supposedly to work for the city.

In later years, by the 1940s, when the financial problems were becoming more systemic and the city did surveys of its operations, it was found that Hamtramck had more city workers per capita than just about any other town. Its expenses were way out of line, especially considering its limited

Jos. Campau Avenue just south of the viaduct was a major industrial center in 1920. Ten years earlier, this was mainly farmland.

revenue. By the 1930s, the city often had to turn to the Dodge factory to seek advance tax payments to stave off payless paydays for city workers.

In October 1929, the financial situation took on a whole new dimension. Monday, October 28, and Tuesday, October 29, saw severe declines in the stock market, which was one of the causes of the Great Depression. In fact, the Great Depression was not an event, it was a series of events— principally the severe western drought leading to the dust bowl, the failure of the banking system, a drop in consumer spending and deflation and a stock market inflated by persons who bought company shares on credit. Few people in Hamtramck owned stocks, so they were not impacted directly by the crash of the stock market, but they did have money in the banks. Not much, but to them it was everything. This was before the Federal Deposit Insurance Corporation (FDIC) was established, so the closing of banks meant the money was gone, for the most part. It also seared into the hearts of many people an everlasting distrust of banks that was so painful that even after the FDIC was created and bank deposits were insured, people would not deposit money in the banks. There are numerous reports of people buying houses in Hamtramck and finding thousands of dollars in cash hidden in the walls, stashed there by previous owners who had lost everything in the bank collapse of the Great Depression.

Ironically, many of the Hamtramck banks were solvent during the "bank holiday" declared by President Franklin Roosevelt and could have stayed open during the crisis. People's State Bank, Joseph Chronowski's Liberty State Bank and the Bank of Hamtramck all survived the Great Depression.

But not all banks did, and their carcasses littered the town, eventually being turned into bowling alleys and bars. They stood as painful reminders of what had been lost. The Great Depression had a domino effect. As people lost money in the banks, they cut back on spending. Demand for goods decreased, and sales slumped. People were laid off, putting an increased strain on what social networks there were as cities tried to provide some degree of welfare. As the number of unemployed increased, sales of all manner of things fell even more. And for an industrial town like Hamtramck, the result was devastating. Auto sales plunged from 5.3 million units in 1920 to fewer than 2.4 million in 1930. The unemployment in town skyrocketed, reaching an estimated mind-numbing 60 percent. Thousands of families went on relief, so much so that the city's resources to help the poor were strained to the limit. Under such circumstances, it's not surprising that so many people turned to manufacturing moonshine—and drinking it.

That's the situation Tenerowicz faced as he moved into his second term. But it wouldn't be long before the woes of the city would be overshadowed by Tenerowicz's personal problems. With no improvement on the crime scene, investigations into the town continued, and in 1932, a Wayne County grand jury indicted Tenerowicz; police chief Harry Wermuskerken; police captain Joseph Rupinski; common councilmen Fred Dibble (remember him?) and Joseph Skomski; and racketeer Joseph Kaplan. It was the same old story: collusion with vice. Specifically, Tenerowicz, Wermuskerken and Rupinski were being paid off monthly to protect the various criminal operations. There was some damning testimony tying Tenerowicz, Rupinski, Wermuskerken and Kaplan directly to the bribery, and it didn't take a jury long to find all four guilty. But charges had been dropped against Dibble and Skomski. Wayne County circuit court judge Homer Ferguson, who probably grew to know more about Hamtramck than anybody considering the Hamtramck corruption trials he presided over, gave them each three and a half to five years in prison.

At the sentencing, Ferguson said, "As mayor, police chief and police captain, three of you certainly knew the enormity of the crime. The citizens of your community placed in your hands the official duty to enforce the law. Democracy expects that he who offers to, and does, represent the people shall be loyal to his trust…you shall have time to meditate on the wrong you have done and the enormity of your crime."

Tenerowicz was not repentant. On his conviction, he resigned from office in a strongly worded, emotional letter to the common council. He wrote:

> *Four years ago, I, a newcomer to the political arena of the city of Hamtramck, was elected your mayor. Two years ago I was re-elected by a tremendous majority of voters of the city.*
>
> *For four years, I believe, I have held the confidence and respect of the residents of this city. In my own heart, I know that every effort has been made by myself to conduct the affairs of my city in an able, honest and conscientious manner.*
>
> *However, I have made enemies, men who have stooped to every possible method no matter how low or unjust, to degrade me and ruin me, not only politically but privately.*
>
> *They have harassed, annoyed and hindered me in every way possible. They have perjured themselves in the courts of this state. They have, at least temporarily, succeeded in their efforts.*
>
> *Although the jury has found me guilty, I feel down deep in my heart, and in the eyes of my maker, that I am innocent of the charges against me. Eventually my vindication will be completely established.*

Tenerowicz stepped aside, and Jezewski reentered the picture, taking over as mayor again. But this was not the end of Tenerowicz. Not even close to the finale.

He and the others didn't just trot off to jail, at least not immediately. The case was appealed, and Tenerowicz went about tending to his patients. Apparently, the conviction didn't cause him the slightest bit of harm among those constituents or anyone else. The appeal lingered until March 1934, when the Michigan Supreme Court upheld the convictions and the defendants were sent to prison.

Until now, this had been a rather familiar story of crime and corruption that had become all too common. Stand by as we are about to enter the world of the surreal. To say that Tenerowicz was well liked in Hamtramck was as much of an understatement as to say that Prohibition was disliked.

That was vividly shown as Tenerowicz headed to the slammer. The *New Deal* newspaper reported on March 23, 1934:

> *Dr. Rudolph G, Tenerowicz, one of Hamtramck's most beloved citizens, one of the city's leading surgeons, and twice mayor of the community, became a convict Thursday.*
>
> *While friends throughout the nation telegraphed entreaties to Governor Comstock for a pardon, the doctor was locked up in a cell at County Jail. Sheriff Thomas Wilcox said he would take Dr. Tenerowicz from the Wayne County Jail and turn him over to the prison authorities Friday noon.*
>
> *Then Wilcox also joined in the plea for a pardon. He said he would invoke the aid of Vice President John N. Garner in securing executive clemency for the doctor.*

Loyalty to Tenerowicz was so fierce that his lawyers were jailed on contempt for refusing to turn him over to the court, saying that would jeopardize their plans to take the case to the U.S. Supreme Court. But that was just the beginning. As he sat in jail, his supporters were out collecting signatures on a petition to present to Governor William Comstock, asking that Tenerowicz be freed. Some ten thousand people signed the petition, which was presented to the governor. Whether party politics played any part in this is uncertain, but the Democratic governor granted the pardon, saying Tenerowicz was the victim "of political revenge." In December 1934, nine months after Tenerowicz stepped into jail, he stepped out.

Tenerowicz was driven home from Jackson Prison by State Representative Michael Grajewski, another Hamtramckan, and there was a party of fifty people waiting for him at his home. "He smilingly greeted well-wishers while his sister-in-law and brother served the gathering with beer and sandwiches," the *New Deal* newspaper reported. (The beer was OK. Remember, Prohibition was over by now. We'll get back to that.)

He had something else to smile about. There was also a brand-new Dodge parked in front of his house when he got home, courtesy of his friends.

Yet Tenerowicz's story was far from done. He would serve another term as mayor of Hamtramck and follow that with two terms in Congress. He seemed nearly impervious to critics. His last term as mayor was marked by a vicious public row with his estranged wife that degenerated into a sordid divorce with him virtually accusing her of being responsible for the death of their two children (they died of tuberculosis) and her charging him with adultery and maintaining a "love nest" on Lake Huron (he did).

Mayor Rudolph Tenerowicz greeted President Franklin Roosevelt when Roosevelt came to dedicate Keyworth Stadium in 1936.

But even when he switched parties and became a Republican, he maintained a loyal following of Democrats in Hamtramck. Not even the powerful United Automobile Workers (UAW) could hurt him when they blasted him for splitting with President Franklin Roosevelt, who was virtually a saint in Hamtramck. Certainly the loyalty was strengthened by the fact that even when he was in Congress, he came home on weekends and maintained his medical practice, still treating patients.

What finally did take him down was the city election of 1948 when he ran for mayor. Although he claimed to live in Hamtramck, records showed that his actual residence was in the upscale Palmer Park neighborhood of Detroit. Through it all, he seemed to take things in stride, but there were signs that it had taken its toll on him. One Christmas he sent out a card with the title "The Joys of a Mayor." Its content consisted of one unbroken paragraph that seemed to sum up his frustration:

> *I have been fussed, mussed, cussed and discussed; Accused, abused and misused; I have been rammed, jammed, slammed and damned; Grieved,*

peeved, relieved and deceived; Helloed, piccaloed and buffaloed; Been called, hauled, bawled, and mauled; Bluffed, puffed, ruffed and cuffed: Nicked, picked, kicked and licked; Been ruled, pooled, tooled and fooled; Racked, whacked, cracked and smacked; Jounced, denounced, flounced and trounced; Have been robbed, dubbed, clubbed and snubbed; Jumped, dumped, bummed; Dimmed, jimmed and trimmed; Been mugged, lugged, tugged and slugged; Docked, rocked, socked and knocked; I have been bodywrecked, Groesbecked, Green and Bruckner-elect; I have been lipped, ripped, zipped, jipped; I have been glad and mad; Been excited, blighted, delighted, righted and indicted; Been called, bawled, stalled and almost recalled. And I have sought, caught, taught and fought for naught. But, for all that, someone has to be MAYOR of Hamtramck.
May Yours be more than a Joyful and Happy Xmas & New Year.
Dr. Rudolph G. Tenerowicz

Tenerowicz died on August 31, 1963, in St. Francis Hospital at age seventy-three. He was buried in Arlington National Cemetery, bringing to an end one of the most colorful careers in the history of Hamtramck politics.

There are still a few Hamtramckans today who can remember skipping rope as a child to the chant, "One-erovich, two-erovich, three-erovich" all the way up to "ten-erovich."

But let's take a step back. The 1920s marked a decade of unprecedented political upheaval and social turmoil in Hamtramck. As the politicians squabbled and gangsters and bootleggers plied their trade, there seemed to be no end in sight for the continuing corruption. The arrival of the Great Depression only made matters worse. In 1932, Jezewski returned to the public scene, with the help of Tenerowicz, and ran successfully for mayor again. But it was the same old sad story. The bootleggers flourished, the feds threatened to take over the town and corruption continued.

However, things were about to change in a big way as the people of Hamtramck looked at ways to combat the crime and corruption and the people of America finally had had enough of Prohibition.

CHAPTER 4

TO THE MOMS!

Consider the moms. They're the ones who had to put up with the drunken husbands. They had to take care of the kids in circumstances that would drive a social worker to drink today. They had to work at home even if they had an outside job, like cleaning someone else's house, for which they were paid pennies. They did the cooking, cleaning, much of the family raising and couldn't even express their views at the polls. This is not to say that the men were shiftless and lazy. Most were extremely hardworking and did not squander their paychecks at the bars and blind pigs. But plenty of them did just that, and it wasn't unusual for mom to send junior to the row of neighborhood bars to find dad and drag him home.

Life is always hard for the poor, but it was brutal during Prohibition, especially during the Great Depression. Most people who bought or rented houses in Hamtramck during those years got only the more meager amenities. Houses came with cold running water and electricity. That was it. No hot water, no furnace, no insulation and the toilet was in the barn out back. Think of how much fun that was at 3:00 a.m. when the temperature was below zero. It was common for people to seal off portions of the house during the winter months because it was too difficult to heat all the rooms. Heating was done with wood-burning stoves, which were replaced with coal-burning furnaces, which in turn gave way to oil and then gas furnaces. Many houses used large gas-fueled heaters equivalent to giant space heaters set in the living room. And there was the kitchen stove. For a long time, it doubled as a furnace to at least heat the kitchen area. Food was basic and mainly

Early developers of Hamtramck Village had no idea of the enormous development that was to occur between 1910 and 1920 when Hamtramck's population went from 3,500 to 48,000.

homemade, including kapusta (fermented cabbage), mushrooms (picked in the forest), home-baked bread, lard (often slathered on the bread) and whatever could be bought at the corner market. And if there was one thing that could challenge the number of bars in town, it was the neighborhood stores. They were almost on every second corner. Family operated, they were the go-to places before supermarkets arrived where you would buy the day-to-day necessities. And for the kids, you could get three pieces of candy for a penny. Never mind if there was blind pig operating in the basement. You could still buy stuff there.

Outperforms every motor car in its price class-Easily!

No need to look far to explain the tremendous success of The Victory Six. It simply outperforms everything in its price class and everybody knows it.

Gets away faster and *goes* faster. Takes the hills faster. Weaves thru traffic faster. Travels faster and smoother over bad roads.

And accelerates faster throughout the entire speed range—5 to 25 miles per hour in 7¼ seconds! 10 to 45 miles in 13½ seconds!

The reason? . . . An engine of amazing flexibility, delivering *more power per pound of car weight than any car in its class!*

Made safe and practical in The Victory by the fine quality of Dodge materials, the high character of Dodge workmanship, and the many new and advanced features of Victory design.

And the smartest, roomiest and most luxurious fine car ever built at The Victory price.

$1095
COUPE-BROUGHAM. F.O.B. DETROIT

The VICTORY SIX

BY DODGE BROTHERS

ALSO THE STANDARD SIX $875 TO $970 AND THE SENIOR SIX $1570 TO $1770

The folks in Hamtramck made the Dodges, but few could afford to buy them. This ad features a new Dodge for $1,095.

To get around, you walked or rode the streetcar if you had to go any distance. Few residents owned cars. Even Henry Ford's most modest models were beyond the reach of nearly all Hamtramckans. The same could be said for the Dodges so many Hamtramckans assembled at the big factory they walked to or took the streetcar to on the south side of town.

With so many houses crammed so close together, Hamtramck was a tight community not only in terms of alcohol consumption but in living space as well. Neighbors were mere feet apart in their individual houses (a situation that remains true today, although the houses have been remodeled and improved).

Looking back, these seem like primitive living conditions, and in many ways they were. Yet they were still vastly better than what the immigrants left back in the Old Country. At least here there was no risk of being drafted into the hated Russian army, which was a reason that prompted many Poles to immigrate to America. Living conditions in Poland—or, for that matter, Germany, Russia or the rural South—were no better there than here, and at least here there were jobs and an opportunity to improve your life. In Poland, landownership was critical to a person's social status. If you didn't own land, you were nobody. In America, ownership was not critical, but it was treasured. That's why Hamtramckans became noted for sweeping the sidewalks and alleys at their homes and maintaining their property. It was part of their heritage. But cleanliness doesn't always go with godliness. And many Hamtramck homes—hundreds, in fact—housed homemade stills in the attics and basements during and even after Prohibition. That was OK. You could make a little money on the side, and what harm was there in brewing up a little something for after dinner or for a wedding or birthday party?

The story was different, though, when the speakeasy down the street, next to the other speakeasy, spilled out drunken sots at two o'clock in the morning. And those ladies on the porch at the house across from yours weren't hanging their laundry out, even though they looked like they were missing some clothes. This kind of activity was common all across town, not just in the seedier sections on the south side near the railroad tracks.

"Bawdy houses flourished," the story in *Follyology* magazine related in 1924. "They operated not only in the by-streets and the main thoroughfares but ran openly in the residential sections. Little children, playing in the streets witnessed the vile solicitations of passing men and on several occasions, it has been brought to light, the older boys themselves were solicited. Young girls, the bloom of girlhood just budding on their cheeks, were enticed into these houses of ill fame."

They called it bathtub gin because it was literally made in a bathtub. The cooker sat on a stove placed in the bathtub, which helped prevent the house from being burned down.

The moms complained to the police. Nothing was done. "Finally a score or more of mothers, enraged at having their children seeing the Bacchanalian revels of these wantons, banded together and armed with broom sticks, stones and other implements of feminine warfare attacked every woman of such character that they could reach within their neighborhood."

It was the moms who helped instigate the cleanup of Hamtramck. Their growing frustration and ferocity spurred the city into finally taking action to help clean up. That wasn't the only time the moms rose up in defiance. Some years later, in 1935, a strong-willed mom named Mary Zuk took control of a mass strike against meat markets in protest of the rising cost of meat. She led that to a national level, even carrying the message to Washington, D.C. At this point, however, malt, not meat, was the object of their derision.

But what to do? There was no sense turning to the police for help. They were worse than useless. Even the state police and the court system had marginal success with dealing with the widespread corruption and law breaking. Help had to come from within from a variety of sources. Some were specifically designed to meet the social needs of the community. Others, like the churches, were pressed into service that extended beyond their spiritual duties. But the movement against the crime and corruption that was ripping the city can be traced to the street level. Not only were the moms upset with the condition of things, but so were a lot of other folks. The African American ministers of the churches in town—and there were several at the time—preached against the evil they saw corrupting their flocks. In 1933, a group calling itself the Committee of Twenty-One issued an open letter demanding the state and county look into the conditions of Hamtramck and remove the politicians in office. "The blind pigs are catering to the young high school girls, which sights are witnessed by the committee are degrading, deplorable and degenerating rat holes for illicit practices which pride and self-respect prohibits writing the description of this matter in detail. The mayor and his appointees have been seen at various times and places gambling for large stakes of money," they wrote. The various authorities took note of the plea and did virtually nothing.

But it was an important step up out of the mire. For the first time, citizens were showing their frustration and objection to what was going on. As has been stated here repeatedly, almost no one liked Prohibition, but what was happening in town went far beyond the effects of liquor. It was bad enough that Hamtramck had a national reputation as a town out of control, but the social problems had a different meaning when they hit home. The gambling, prostitution, thievery and other crimes were affecting the quality of life. Gangsters operated openly and seemed to be supported by the city officials. Who wanted to live in a place like that?

But there were outlets that helped to clean up the town, even if they weren't trying to do just that. One of these was Tau Beta. This was one of the most remarkable social organizations to be found anywhere in the country. What makes it even more amazing is that it was founded by four Detroit girls: Eloise Jenks, Margaret Snow, Hilda Meigs and Marian Stinchfield. Meigs was sixteen and the other three were fifteen in 1901 when they decide to form a club. All four came from well-to-do families, and the club they formed was typical of what upper-class kids would do at that time. Naming themselves the Tau Beta Club, they didn't do much of anything significant at first. They met each Friday, sang songs and designed a special pin for each member to wear. They held parties and dances and played sports, but that was about it. It was all rather exclusive and trivial. Just how exclusive was shown in that as the group grew, the age requirement to be a member was lowered because so many members were being lost as they were shipped off to boarding school.

Mildred Plumb in *The History of Tau Beta*, published in 1938, noted, "Friday afternoons were practically always devoted to a meeting; business the first Friday, specials on the others. There was the business of arranging a dance, banquet or annual group photograph after the society was a going concern. Specials were perhaps to discuss a girl, more often just to get together, practice the new songs or get good 'part singing' into familiar ones." This was not the stuff of greatness and seems utterly quaint and snobbish today. But the little Tau Betans—who also liked to be known as The Bunch, which they cleverly thought played a double meaning for their initials—were adept at fundraising and attracting new members. That's a winning combination for any organization, so through the years, it grew. Operations took on a more serious tone on June 11, 1906, when Tau Beta members "decided to investigate various charities in the city that it might be decided by November 1st what particular charitable work should be selected for the following year."

The girls settled on operating a kitchen for the Visiting Nurse Association. They would prepare food for the ill persons who were treated in their homes by the visiting nurses. The girls cooked the meals and delivered them to the patients. "All delivering was done on streetcar and afoot, just as the nurses themselves went to the patients. A year or so later, when only one or two girls had the use of their family's electrics [cars] we thought ourselves in clover if we were lucky enough to be assigned to trundle about on our calls at all of fifteen miles per hour. Gasoline cars went faster, but very few girls drove them until 1910 or 1911, so the occasional use of Serena Murphy's limousine was a real high spot. Her chauffeur, Max, could get us over so much ground that we might be through by four o'clock, in time for tea at the home of one of the squad members," a member recalled.

The service was successful and expanded through the years. In July 1915, Tau Beta linked up with the Babies' Milk Fund, an organization that helped needy mothers and had a dispensary in Hamtramck. "Polish mothers brought their babies to the Babies' Milk Fund dispensary for medical advice and instructions in care and feeding, all greatly needed." Soon the Tau Beta girls were giving cooking lessons. But what they saw around them was appalling. Hamtramck was in the midst of its phenomenal growth spurt, as it had become the fastest-growing town in America. Neighborhoods were being thrown up at a furious rate. Builders wanted to maximize space and profits, so houses were crammed together. No thought was given to recreation or aesthetics. Virtually all the houses were being occupied as fast as they were being built by poor Polish immigrants, many of whom could barely speak English. Poverty was rampant, and the village government was overwhelmed by the situation. And

SOCIAL PIONEERING

THE STORY OF THE
TAU BETA ASSOCIATION

DETROIT, MICH.
1926

Hamtramck School
and
Public Library

THROUGH THIS DOOR MORE
THAN 2000 PEOPLE PASS
EACH WEEK TO PARTICIPATE
IN TAU BETA ACTIVITIES

Tau Beta Community House, Hamtramck

The Tau Beta Community House served as a counterbalance to the corruption of
Prohibition. It offered social services and programs that benefited the community.

this was even before Prohibition contributed its brand of poison to the mix. Seeing the desperate need around them, the Tau Beta girls decided to open a settlement house in the village and rented a flat on Hanley Street.

The Tau Beta history recounted:

> *Our neighbors in Hamtramck called our new home "the house with the light," and that beacon nightly at our door was its sole distinguishing feature. Cheaply constructed houses and duplexes were springing up in dozens on unpaved streets. There were, for a long time after we entered the community, large numbers of vacant lots, but there were no playgrounds. The school system was undeveloped, the village government had little vision of the public's needs, and naturally was in no hurry to supply what it did not recognize as essential. We aimed to undertake what the authorities did not, or could not, provide and demonstrate its value until the village council would assume any such burden, relieving us to supply other facilities, until we could eventually wish those, too, unto the council, the schools, or whoever should by rights carry their responsibility.*

Tau Beta's first act was to provide dinners for six families, along with baby socks and mittens. Neighbors at first were suspicious. Many had been exploited on their long journey from the Old Country and were not accustomed to strangers bearing gifts. But they soon warmed up to the Tau Betans, especially as they began to offer classes in sewing, cooking, music, singing and gardening. The Tau Beta ladies also began to perform other desperately needed services, including calling doctors, helping with insurance issues and legal matters and supplying food baskets to the needy. Soon, Tau Beta had outgrown its flat and needed more space, so the ladies went house hunting. That in itself was a telling experience. They contacted a Realtor who apparently was bewildered that such well-bred, obviously well-off ladies were looking for a house in Hamtramck. "Ladies, you wouldn't want to live in Hamtramck," he said. "You wouldn't want to live here."

While they didn't want to live there, that is exactly where they wanted their settlement house to be because that is where the need was greatest. Unhappy with all the properties they saw, the ladies decided to build their own Community House and quickly raised the needed money. By then, Tau Beta had attracted attention from some high-profile persons like Eleanor Ford and Howard B. Bloomer, chairman of the board of directors of the Dodge Brothers auto company, who recognized the valuable service it was performing. He showed the company's appreciation by presenting Tau Beta with a check for nearly $12,000 to pay off the mortgage on the new building. Ground was broken for the new settlement house in October 1919, and it was occupied by the following July. The space there allowed Tau Beta to continue expanding its services, including founding the Hamtramck Public Library, opening a child's clinic, sending kids to summer camp and establishing one of the first playgrounds in Hamtramck next to the settlement house. Internally, programs continued to be expanded as Tau Beta became a moving force in Hamtramck.

By 1922, "We had acquired a reputation as go-getters, which stood us in good stead. When we needed funds, we could borrow; our credit was good for 'character loans,' and they said of us in Detroit's financial district, 'Those girls can accomplish anything they set out to do,'" Plumb wrote. That reputation served them well in the next few years as the Tau Beta ladies had even bigger plans. To this time, most of their programs had been geared toward women and girls, but they saw the need for a wider scope of programs that reached out to males. They began a major fundraising program with the aim of building a larger Community House. Working in cooperation with some other metro Detroit social organizations in a grand fundraising campaign, Tau Beta managed to secure $200,000—an impressive sum for the mid-1920s. With that, work began on March 28, 1928, on an expansive building. On June 15 of that year, Tau Beta president Sally Macauley Wadsworth and Mayor Rudolph Tenerowicz helped lay the cornerstone. "The Boy Scouts, with banners and band, marched to the scene of the event, and the city officials and other prominent Hamtramck citizens were present. Movies were taken and the band brought us to our feet for the Star Spangled Banner, and that was one more star-spangled day for our society," Plumb recounted. With the new space open, the Community House staff was expanded to sixteen full-time workers, including four janitors and nine part-time music teachers. In addition, the Visiting Nurse Association occupied the clinic in the building with nine full-time nurses and three part-time doctors. And there was a large staff of volunteers.

Tau Beta's Hamtramck operations were well established as Prohibition went into effect, and while the Community House did not directly have any contact with Prohibition, it did deal with its effects, just as it dealt with almost all the social issues that arose. But one area that connected the two was juvenile delinquency. That was becoming a huge issue in Hamtramck as the general moral structure of the town nearly collapsed during the Prohibition years, and it was one that Tau Beta wanted to focus on.

An array of juvenile gangs roamed Hamtramck, from the Moran gang on the north side of town to the Leuschner gang near the Dodge Main plant. Some had a more formal structure than others, and they were involved in all manner of crimes, from petty theft to robbery. Hamtramck's abundance of railroad lines and rail yards was especially attractive to young thieves who could find easy access to boxcars loaded with valuable metals that could be stolen and sold. Nearly one thousand cases of juvenile delinquency were reported in Hamtramck between 1927 and 1931. That's scarcely surprising considering the economic and social problems of the town. Alcoholism and poverty undermine the family structure, which leads to neglect of the children who can find themselves without the physical and emotional support of the parents. So the kids look elsewhere for support, which they can find in the gangs.

Tau Beta stated:

> *Tau Beta pointed out the "gang spirit" can be good when it is channeled correctly, as in that organization. But when the "gang spirit" develops along the wrong lines, trouble follows. There's always some of it in Hamtramck, as in all large and crowded towns. That is when our staff has had heartbreaking experiences. Boys whom we might have kept from harm, had we been able to get and keep hold on them, as did bad companions, have become serious delinquents. Help for these boys and their sorrowing families is all in the day's work of the staff. Prevention of delinquency is our ideal, and great is our joy when it is achieved.*

One way Tau Beta fought delinquency was with its "Caddy Camp." Opened on Gaukler Pointe, the site of the Edsel Ford Mansion on Lake St. Clair just north of Detroit, the camp offered a respite for boys away from the grimy, crowded, smoky city streets. The boys worked as caddies at a nearby country club to pay their way through the seven-week program. Tau Beta also sponsored recreational activities at the Community House, including amateur acting productions starring local youths. How much of an impact this made is impossible to measure, but long after Tau Beta closed its Hamtramck operations in 1957, those who took part in its programs remembered it with reverence. Some even said it turned their lives around. Tau Beta closed its Hamtramck operations, saying that by that time it could offer nothing more than the city could through its recreational and social programs. Tau Beta gracefully bowed off the stage after an enormously satisfying performance.

Tau Beta wasn't the only organization trying to bring some order to the community's chaos. The Hamtramck Public School District started modestly with a few scattered one-room schoolhouses designed to serve a mainly rural community. One of these, Holbrook School, was built in the 1890s and served as the core of the evolving Hamtramck School District, which was reorganized from a primary township district to a graded school district in

Somehow throughout all the turmoil of Prohibition and the Great Depression, Hamtramck students managed to receive a first-rate education in some state-of-the-art buildings.

June 1897. The original wooden Holbrook School building was replaced with a brick structure at that time and was expanded in 1905 and 1913. With the explosive growth of Hamtramck in the second decade of the twentieth century, the demands on the schools grew tremendously.

As thousands of immigrant kids flooded into the district, the need for additional school buildings became more pronounced. In 1913, the Dickinson family donated land occupied by their farm for the site of the new Dickinson School. In 1915, the combination junior and senior high school was built, although the junior section was opened first, with the high school side opening a year later. The junior and senior high school operations were conducted in two separate buildings connected by a second-story covered corridor. A vocational school building on the campus separated from the two joined buildings was added in 1924. In 1917, Whitney School—which later became Pulaski School—was built.

And there would be even more: in quick succession, Playfair, Pulaski and Kosciuszkio schools were built. Even as those were being built, the others were being expanded, often several times. The numbers were growing staggering. In the 1920s, for example, attendance at Hamtramck High School went from 937 to 1,870 in the space of three years. All the schools, in fact, faced similar if somewhat less dramatic growth. Still, the growth rate was almost alarming, with more than 10,000 children in the public schools by the early 1920s.

E.G. van Deventer was school superintendent at this time, and although those who knew him referred to him as competent, he was much too conservative to deal successfully with the rapid changes taking place. Not only were these children pouring into the school district, but they were also difficult to educate. Many did not speak English. They had health problems. They had dental problems and psychiatric issues. They were being raised in traumatic conditions in poverty-stricken families. It was common for students to drop out of school to work in the factories as soon as they could, even if they had to lie about their age. The law said they had to attend school full time at least until they were sixteen and part time until they were seventeen. But the actual numbers showed a significant drop in attendance in the higher grade levels. In 1920, for every one hundred kids in the fifth grade, there were two in the twelfth grade. Although the dropout rate in Michigan was much higher than even nationally, Hamtramck's rate was particularly dismal. Detroit, for example, had twenty-one kids in twelfth grade for every one hundred in fifth grade in 1925.

A 1925 survey of the students done by the school district showed that 65 percent who left school went to work in factories. But how many simply ended up on the dusty streets of the town? Or in the pool halls? Or drifting into petty theft? Or running booze for bootleggers? Or worse?

Juvenile delinquency became a major problem in the city that persisted all the way through Prohibition and into the Great Depression. Some cases were just mischief, kids getting into trouble like kids often do. But as the depths of the Depression increased, so did the seriousness of the trouble. For example, four kids, ages fourteen, fifteen, fourteen and eighteen, stole a stamp machine from a store. The owner recognized them and told the cops. In another case, two teens, ages sixteen and seventeen, admitted they broke into a candy store and stole ten dollars in cash. They also broke into some houses where they stole cigarettes and clothes that they sold to a store. The store owner was charged with receiving stolen property. In yet another instance, four young men, ranging in ages from eighteen to twenty-one, admitted to holding up a man and getting away with thirty-one dollars in cash and the man's car. He said they also beat him and attempted to fire a gun at his head. They said they only got two dollars and only slapped him and never intended to shoot him, just scare him. Even worse, nine juveniles got into a fight with a man attending a wedding. As fists

flew, he fell over and hit his head on a railing, fracturing his skull. He died.

This was serious stuff and just a few examples of many reports. Clearly, something had to be done. But the schools, like the village and early city, were being overwhelmed by the scope of the problem. Just finding space to place students in the school buildings was a challenge. Class sizes were unacceptable by today's standards. Typically, elementary classes held 45 students. Junior high accommodated 35 to 45 students per class, and this could be expanded up to 120 students in music and health classes. Senior high classes were to be limited to 35 students. The district was fairly able to adhere to these numbers by enlarging the buildings and adding new ones when it could, but the challenges still remained.

The answer came in the form of Dr. Maurice Keyworth. A product of Michigan, Keyworth was named superintendent of the Hamtramck Public Schools in 1923. He knew what he was getting into and recognized that if the schools were to succeed, a whole new approach to education was needed. So he set about redesigning the school system, expanding the focus beyond education to meet the needs of these particular children. He laid out his philosophy in a research document called "Housing the Children—A Community Project." This was released in 1926, a year before he would prepare the new school code, which was even more of a landmark work.

School superintendent Maurice Keyworth was a brilliant educator who brought national acclaim to the Hamtramck Public Schools.

TO THE MOMS!

In "Housing the Children," he wrote, "The democratic administration of a school system means full participation, under leadership, of every individual in the school system in every activity. The welfare of the community is so closely bound to the welfare of the schools that every school project further requires the active cooperation of every member of the community." That was a major element of Keyworth's approach: involve everyone. Make everyone a stakeholder in education—the students, the teachers, the administrators, the parents, even the janitors, who had a role in keeping conditions in the buildings conducive for learning. Everyone had a hand in the educational process, and they were not only advised but even required to take part in the educational process.

A fundamental problem that Keyworth recognized immediately was the language barrier. How do you teach a child when you can't talk to him or her? There are anecdotal stories of kids coming home from school complaining that they were told they were going to have to learn a new language: English. So Keyworth instituted bilingual education, and not just for the children. He fostered a wildly successful adult education program. Although there were thousands of students in the classrooms during the day, there were even more adults there at night. Keyworth also instituted a program of issuing school bulletins that were sent home to the parents so they would have an understanding of what was going on in the schools. Parents were encouraged to understand what their children were learning in school, and it was demanded that parents send their kids to school. If the kids were absent, someone from the schools would be knocking on their door asking about the child.

For those with special needs, doctors and dentists were brought into the school buildings. They helped identify and treat a wide range of problems the kids had. Remember, these were immigrant kids who came from poverty either here or in the Old Country. Many had never seen a doctor before. And this was a time when diseases like polio and tuberculosis were much more prevalent. Children suffering from the effects of polio and other debilitating muscular diseases were treated in special therapeutic pools installed in the schools where paralyzed and stunted limbs could be exercised. Kids suffering from respiratory illnesses could take advantage of "Open Window Rooms." As the name implies, these were rooms with large windows that could be opened so the kids could relax in a sedate, comforting atmosphere. Other special rooms were set aside for treating kids with hearing, orthopedic and vision problems and for those labeled as "slow learners." These children were also given hot lunches, and they received yearly physical examinations. Keyworth also brought in social workers to help identify kids with emotional problems and scars at the Psychological

Clinic that was established in 1926. Keyworth did not invent special education, but he refined it in the Hamtramck schools.

The schools even established the recreation program for the city after the government failed to meet the need. The Department of Recreation was organized in February 1925, opening nine school gyms in seven school buildings for public use. Soon baseball, basketball, softball and basketball leagues were formed. The school playgrounds were opened for the community, as were the school pools. Other activities—including tennis, dancing, badminton, boxing, wrestling and weightlifting, among others—were offered, along with less strenuous activities like chess, checkers, table tennis and reading.

The system was so successful that the Little League baseball team won the world championship in 1959 followed by the Pony League world championship in 1962. But world crowns weren't contemplated in the 1920s when the recreation program began. The aim was to provide healthy outlets for the kids to keep them out of trouble. At one point, Mayor Rudolph Tenerowicz teamed up with local tennis coach Jean Hoxie to start a tennis program for youths at risk of becoming delinquent. Hoxie was the right person to ask. She would become world famous for her tennis-teaching skills. She trained players like Jane "Peaches" Bartkowicz and Fred Kovaleski at Hamtramck Veterans Memorial Park. They would go on to become Wimbledon champions. Kovaleski, in fact, continued playing tennis well into his nineties, winning tournaments around the world.

(As a sidelight, I can't let this pass without noting that after Kovaleski won at Wimbledon in 1950, he turned pro. He played primarily in Europe and North Africa. However, while he was a great tennis player, that was just his cover. His real job was being a spy for the CIA.)

Keyworth also wanted to address another aspect of student development that he felt was critical: Americanization. Here he would take an approach that was as ingenious as it was effective. First, he stressed to the kids and their parents the value of American society. For most of the immigrants, democracy was a foreign concept. They understood the nature of freedom, but few had experienced it under the oppressive rule of governments back in

Opposite, top: The Hamtramck Recreation Department was formed in 1927. Thirty-two years later, it produced the world champion Little League baseball team.

Opposite, bottom: Tennis was used as a tool to fight delinquency, and Jean Hoxie was its leading proponent. She trained Wimbledon champions at Veterans Memorial Park. With her are Dick Russell and Johnny Koliba (in front of net) and Al Hetzeck and Walter English.

Europe. Keyworth sought to instill in them the concept that they were Americans now and should adapt to American ways, especially in loyalty to the American system. But he understood the link they had with their customs, culture and ethnic heritage, and he did not try to change that. In fact, he built on it. Seeing that so many of the immigrants were Polish, he renamed Whitney School as Pulaski School. Playfair School became Pilsudski School. When he built the junior high school in 1931, he called it Copernicus Junior High School. The same was true for Kosciuszko School. All were given names of Polish heroes that any Pole would relate to. Keyworth's message was simple but effective: cherish your culture and heritage and live it at home. But remember, you are now saluting the American flag. You are Americans.

It worked splendidly. In a matter of a few years, Hamtramck's school system began to receive national recognition. The school code, in fact, was adopted to some degree by school districts across America. Even today, the 260-page document has a quality of freshness about it that is striking. It reads as if it could have been written yesterday.

Keyworth attained national recognition and in 1935 was elected the state superintendent of public instruction. He clearly was destined for greater things at the highest levels of education, but he never achieved them. Why? Just weeks after he was elected to the state post, he was visiting schools in Michigan's Upper Peninsula when his car was struck by another car. He died in the crash. All of Hamtramck was in shock. His body was brought back to town and laid in state at Hamtramck High School. A line of thousands of people, including educators from across Michigan, came by to bid a final farewell.

It's easy statistically to measure Keyworth's impact on schools. The number of high school seniors increased every year. Some students were even going to college. Consider Emil Konopinski. He graduated from Hamtramck High School in 1929, destined to work at the Dodge Main factory. But Principal E.M. Conklin had other plans for him. He went to the Hamtramck Rotary Club and got Konopinski a full scholarship to the University of Michigan. Konopinski became a key scientist in the development of the atomic bomb and conducted critical research into the atomic bomb by showing that detonating it would not set the earth's atmosphere on fire, as had been feared. Konopinski had a long career that included being a professor of physics at Indiana University, and he was recognized as a great physicist.

Along with the public schools, several parochial schools were established in Hamtramck. St. Florian Parish created a grade school in 1909, and St. Ladislaus and Our Lady Queen of Apostles Parishes would follow suit in later years. Immaculate Conception Ukrainian Catholic Parish also would establish an elementary and high school in later years. But their situation was somewhat different. They were religious-based with a strong code of discipline and a rigid ethic. If you didn't comply, you were out. It was as simple as that. Troublemakers were given little leeway. Unlike the public schools, the Catholic schools could be selective in choosing who they let in and kept in—and they let in a lot. By 1923, the three-story St. Florian School building, which covers a corner of a block (it's still there), housed an astounding 2,500 students. But religious education was important to many parents, and no doubt the schools would have had even more students if their parents had been able to pay the required tuition, modest as it was.

There's no way of determining what impact the religious schools may have had on the juvenile delinquency rate, but it likely wasn't great. Temptation still abounded on the streets outside the school buildings. And while a kid might go to church six days a week, as was common, the pool halls were open all the time. And they were just a step away from the speakeasies and houses of ill repute.

But providing another set of balances, smaller social organizations also took root in the city. St. Anne's Community House on Andrus Street offered a variety of programs and served as the meeting place of numerous groups, somewhat like Tau Beta did, but on a much smaller scale. The granddaddy of all social organizations in Hamtramck, the Hamtramck Indians, also sought to improve the quality of life. Formed in the 1890s, the Indians were the first social organization to be formed in the city with the goal "to aid, assist and help the fellow man." Over the years, the group raised money for various charities. Ironically, it was founded by a group of saloonkeepers, and it regularly met in the space above Cooper's saloon on Jos. Campau Avenue.

Membership in the Hamtramck Indians was quite exclusive and limited to residents who had to be nominated for membership. But there were other clubs that were less rigorous to join, like the Bon Ton Club, the Galaxy Club, the Dandies Club, the Exchange Club, the Cameo Club, the Firebird Amateur Radio Club and many, many more. The churches also hosted a variety of organizations, ostensibly religiously based, like the Dads' Club, the Ushers' Club, St. Theresa's Guild and many more, which served as social organizations at least as much as religiously oriented ones. The idea in all of them was to provide a healthy outlet for people of all ages to do constructive things. Not every man wanted to squander his money in a bar or at a blind pig. Many folks had good family lives and didn't appreciate the hookers hanging out on the porches. They were interested in building decent neighborhoods free of crime. But with the political situation in constant

The caption of this telling cartoon from the *Dziennik Polski* (*Polish Daily News*) basically says, "When you're done there, come see us."

turmoil, there was little hope of making substantial progress against the tide of sin so prevalent in town.

That changed beginning in 1933 as the city, and the entire nation, was about to take a big step forward in fighting the forces of drink by—of all things—embracing it.

CHAPTER 5

TO THE BOOTLEGGERS!

And so it ended. The Twenty-first Amendment to the U.S. Constitution, repealing the Eighteenth Amendment, was ratified by the state of Utah, bringing an end to Prohibition on December 5, 1933. Happy days were here again.

Even some of the bootleggers were pleased. As Mayor Joseph Lewandowski remembered some years later, "They were the only ones with the money." And they had the knowledge and at least some of the infrastructure to brew legally. Some previous legal brewers who had been forced out of business by Prohibition got back into the act. C&K Brewing Company spent the Prohibition years producing liquid malt, which was legal. When Prohibition ended, owner Casimir Kocat wanted to retire and move to Florida, so he sold his Hamtramck brewery for $158,000, a tidy sum in the depths of the Great Depression. In its first year of operation, 1934, the new owners of C&K sold thirty-seven thousand barrels of beer, which was a decent number. Alas, C&K's initial success did not last. Without Kocat, the investors who took over the company somehow just couldn't connect with the public. Despite some product changes, sales dropped, and the brewery closed in 1936. The building still stands, however, between Sobieski and Klinger Streets.

Auto City was operated by Joseph Chronowski and his brother Stanislav. Joseph dropped out of the operations when Prohibition was adopted in Michigan and founded Liberty State Bank. Stanislav continued to run the place for a few years more after switching the product line to soft drinks. That

Left: Casmir Kocat offers a tempting glass of beer from his C&K Brewery that reopened as soon as Prohibition ended in 1933.

Below: The C&K Brewery building still survives, on Klinger Street just north of Casmere Street. It stopped producing beer in 1936.

A view of the C&K Brewery shows an apparently older section. There are still small buildings in town that once served as distribution outlets for the breweries.

didn't last long, however, and the building was leased to a relative who started brewing beer again, Prohibition notwithstanding. Eventually, the feds caught up with him, and off he went to Leavenworth (which seemed to be becoming a second home for Hamtramckans by this time). In 1928, the brothers took over the plant again and started making malt. They were doing that when Prohibition ended, so it was an easy matter for them to switch over to the real thing. They renovated the brew house and began producing beer in 1934 and did all right for a while. But the auto industry strikes of 1937 had a major impact on sales. The Hamtramck Dodge Main plant, in particular, was the site of a massive sit-down strike that closed operations, and it was just part of a larger series of auto industry strikes. Facing a 36 percent drop in sales in 1937, the brewery was knocked into a downward spiral from which it could not recover. It closed in 1941.

The end of Prohibition was something to toast, and people did just that. The State Liquor Control Commission reported in 1935 that the city's pre-Easter liquor sales were the third highest in the state. More than $4,000 was spent on liquor at the city's state liquor store on the Saturday before Easter. The store served some 2,814 patrons that day, store manager Joseph Wisniewski said. "But no one had to wait more than ten minutes," he said. "The patience and orderliness of the buyers facilitated matters and relieved congestion." As impressive as those numbers were, it did not compare to the $6,700 that had been spent on the previous New Year's Eve.

All this makes it seem hard to realize there was still a Great Depression going on then. But there was, just as there was little else to dull the pain of poverty. The nation was still deep in the clutches of the economic downturn, and Hamtramck, with its strong connection to industry, was hit extremely hard. Unemployment skyrocketed, and with little money to spend in the bars, many folks continued to make and sell their own liquor illegally well past the end of Prohibition.

In August 1935, police received a phone call directing them to a house on Charest Avenue where they uncovered a twenty-five-gallon still, two gallons of moonshine and four barrels of mash. In January 1936, a twenty-eight-year-old Hamtramck man was charged with violating federal laws for operating an illegal still. And these were not isolated incidents. Nearly every issue of the weekly local newspaper had some account of an illegal still being busted somewhere or a gambling ring smashed or hookers hauled into court.

To make it worse, the air of corruption remained pervasive, and not just in the sale of booze. In March 1935, Charles G. Lockwood, counsel for the County Consumer Council, came to the Hamtramck Common Council to complain that the big area creameries were putting the squeeze on the local distributors, forcing small merchants to jack up their prices to an exorbitant level. "Dealers can make a handsome profit by selling milk at 12 cents a quart," Lockwood said.

The political climate also remained foul. Jezewski won reelection in 1932 and presided over the end of Prohibition. During this period, Tenerowicz had finally been shuffled off to prison as his appeals for his earlier conviction

A genuine, complete illegal still is housed in the modern Hamtramck Historical Museum. It was found in the basement of a building in Hamtramck.

were exhausted. But corruption continued unabated across town, and the sense of frustration among the residents was growing. Voices of change rose, like the so-called Committee of Twenty-one, which appealed to state and county officials to come in and clean up Hamtramck once and for all. The local politicians were threatened—once again—but nothing came of it. Amid this turmoil, a "new" political face arose on the scene. Joseph Lewandowski was appointed assistant city attorney in 1928. He was hardly a newcomer to the political scene; he had been Tenerowicz's campaign manager and delivered speeches for him. But they had a major parting of the way when Tenerowicz was elected and appointed all his pals to some job or another—except Lewandowski. "Everybody was appointed but me," Lewandowski recounted years later.

Despite being sour over the lack of an appointment, Lewandowski maintained that he ran for office "to help the people." A successful attorney, Lewandowski said that being mayor paid $5,000. Yet he was making $60,000 on his own. "Why take a $5,000 job?" he questioned. "I wanted to help people." He also noted that in those days, a spirited campaign cost $50,000 to run. That was

Mayor Joseph Lewandowski fought a bitter political battle against Rudolph Tenerowicz, his one-time ally. Lewandowski won one term but couldn't gain a second.

an astronomical sum at that time and brought into question the motivation of many candidates. The implication, of course, was that a person in the right position could make a lot more money than the salary provided through bribes and kickbacks.

In the 1934 election, Lewandowski prevailed over Jezewski, who promptly announced he was leaving public life and would concentrate on his pharmacy thereafter. He died in 1960 after suffering a heart attack while walking on Jos. Campau, just a short distance from his pharmacy.

Installed in office, Lewandowski embarked on a program to put people to work. "I can't be happy as mayor of Hamtramck if my people are unemployed," he said. "It's up to me. It's up to all of us to get as many people back to work as possible." With that, he started a registration program for all unemployed persons with the goal of getting a job for one member of every family. Thousands applied. That was in April 1934. By August, only four people had gotten jobs. Lewandowski went to the common council to explain the shortfall and told them that he had written to Senator Arthur H. Vandenberg, but Vandenberg replied he could not do anything to help. Lewandowski recommended the city write to Walter P. Chrysler and ask him to employ Hamtramckans. "We ought to put all the people to work and make manufacturers pay for it in taxes," Lewandowski said.

The council did not agree. "We shouldn't talk like that," Councilman Constantine Cetlinski said. "We should use tact with them. After all, they are the ones who are giving jobs."

This did not bode well for the Lewandowski administration. Neither did the unabated crime. It was the same old story. Corruption was flourishing, some of it right under Lewandowski's nose—literally. "They would move right next door to you," he said of a brothel that opened near his Holbrook Avenue home. "I never knew there was a house of ill repute next door—and I was mayor. There was nothing you could do." Well, maybe in general, but as to that particular house, "I took care of that in a hurry," Lewandowski said.

But seemingly, he didn't take care of much else, at least on the crime front, although he noted ironically, "Under my administration not only the alleys but the streets were kept in perfect cleanliness, and I feel proud of the fact that I was the first mayor to inaugurate cleanliness in our city." Indeed, the city did win a number of national awards for being the cleanest in the nation during this period. The streets certainly were clean, but what was happening on them was less pristine. In November 1935, Lewandowski was forced to take action. In response to a series of articles that appeared in the *Detroit Free Press*, Lewandowski made headlines of his own when he ordered Police Commissioner Stephen A. Majewski (remember him?) to "crash into every gambling place you seriously suspect as a gambling house or house of ill repute. Smash the paraphernalia, furniture and windows. If I find one case where this order is violated, I'll start firing," he said. "I have adopted this sweeping police order to show that Hamtramck can be a model city and because I shall not rest until the only kind of publicity Hamtramck can get is good publicity. I am convinced the taxpayers here want an immaculately clean city at any cost."

What raised Lewandowski's ire was comprehensiveness of the *Free Press* stories. They charged, among other things, that three gambling houses were operating on Jos. Campau across from the Dodge Main factory; a building at 7631 Jos. Campau had eight gambling tables; two other gambling places were so bold as to have persons on the street ushering customers in; one of the biggest blind pigs in town was at 11360 Jos. Campau, above an auto dealership; a gambling place was located just below Mayor Stephen Majewski's second-floor law office; and a Hamtramck police officer was overseeing a chain of five "resorts" that employed fifty women.

Majewski said he didn't know anything about the alleged blind pig below, and Lewandowski went on the attack. "Instead of scandalizing the good name of Hamtramck and using this city as a political football, the commissioner or I should have been told about anything that may have been wrong here and I certainly would have seen to it that the situation was corrected immediately," he said. His stance was supported by a coalition of Hamtramck groups called the Inter-Organization of Hamtramck, which released a statement attacking the *Free Press*. The statement read:

> We wish to point out that the articles calling attention to alleged vice conditions in Hamtramck were unjust, in that they grossly misrepresented

the condition and tend to mislead the general public into believing that organized vice is tolerated in the city of Hamtramck. In justice to our citizens, the article should have pointed out that neither the Prosecuting Attorney nor the Sheriff of Wayne County has found any cause to complain about the conditions here, nor the lack of cooperation. It should have been made clearer that the Prosecuting Attorney admits that all complaints forwarded by him to the police department were acted upon promptly, and that since August of this year, the Prosecutor's Office had received only two complaints, both of which were acted upon.

If it is intended to give the public a true picture of Hamtramck as it is today, we would recommend sending representatives to our city to verify the unquestioned fact that Hamtramck has cleaner streets and alleys than any other city of its size in Michigan, a fact of which we are justly proud, and which deserves proper mention in newspapers.

Among the groups making up the Inter-Organization Committee were the Citizens Protective League, the Civic Club of St. Ladislaus Parish, the Ukrainian-American Citizens Club, the Thaddeus Kosciuszko Democratic Club of Hamtramck and the Alliance of Poles and the Slovak Club, among others.

The result of all of this? Nothing.

Periodic raids continued as before, but vice went on seemingly pretty much unchecked. In February 1936, the Wilhelm Hotel was busted for gambling. Police raided the place at 6:00 p.m. on a Friday and found about sixty men, mainly factory workers, inside. About half of them ran out ahead of the police and escaped. Some twenty-five were arrested, and two were charged with running an illegal operation. Still, Lewandowski was beginning to feel the heat. And a lot of it was coming from our old friend Dr. Rudolph Tenerowicz, who was back on the political scene after being pardoned from prison by the governor.

The approaching election of April 1936 was shaping up to be a hot one. Some 19,463 people registered to vote—the largest number ever recorded in the city. Lewandowski ran on the slogan "Keep the man and keep the plan." This was "a call to decency and a call to back the man who had done more than any other mayor to give Hamtramck a better name in the eyes of the whole United States." Perhaps. But a turn in prison had done nothing to reduce the solid support Tenerowicz had gained in the community. Even when the situation took a bizarre turn in late March 1936 and someone blew up a bomb outside Lewandowski's window, Tenerowicz knew how to respond.

TO THE BOOTLEGGERS!

No one was hurt in the blast, but it did shake up the family. Lewandowski immediately offered a $500 reward for anyone with information about the perpetrator of the blast. Just as quickly, Tenerowicz offered his own $500 reward, but an intensive investigation failed to turn up anything.

When the election was held in April, Tenerowicz was "vindicated" in his eyes for whatever transgressions he may have committed, as he easily defeated Lewandowski. Tenerowicz drew 7,637 votes to Lewandowski's 6,476. Regarding city affairs, Tenerowicz's term in office was relatively uneventful. It was during his tenure that the city built Keyworth Stadium, which was dedicated by President Franklin Roosevelt, who delivered a speech there in October 1936. There still was vice, there still was corruption. There still were stills, but this didn't rise to the level of previous years. Tenerowicz's problems were mainly personal as he got into a huge fight with his estranged wife, from whom he wanted a divorce. Their squabbling took on the drama of a soap opera as they battled out their differences on the front pages of the newspapers. Mrs. Tenerowicz went so far as to expose his dalliances with another woman at a "love nest" he built along the shore of Port Huron.

But Doc Ten was unfazed. He ran for reelection in 1938 facing his old nemesis Joseph Lewandowski. Lewandowski had had his own trouble with the law and was charged with collusion with the bootleggers, but he was acquitted after a six-week trial. Against Tenerowicz, Lewandowski ran a blistering campaign, accusing Tenerowicz of all manner of transgressions. He even published his own newspaper, the *Hamtramck News*, which was devoted to tearing down Tenerowicz. (This form of campaigning was common in this period. A lot of politicians put out their own "newspapers.") Just before the election, on Sunday, April 3, 1938, the *Hamtramck News* blazed with the double-deck headline "Citizens Demand Tenerowicz's Removal from City Hall." Below that was another double-deck headline proclaiming "Attorney Joseph A. Lewandowski Will Return Good Name to Our City."

The accompanying story read:

> *Our city of which we should be proud has lately become infested again with gambling houses and dens of vice. These establishments are open day and night. Bloody murders are frequent occurrences there. The fact is that in a certain gambling house on Jos. Campau Avenue within a stone's throw from the city hall, two weeks ago again one man was killed and two injured at 5:45 in the morning!*
>
> *It is a fact that a twenty-one year old young man was murdered in another gambling house on Caniff Avenue at 4 o'clock in the morning.*

Mayor Joseph Lewandowski ripped into former Mayor Rudolph Tenerowicz when they ran against each other for mayor. Lewandowski produced this campaign newspaper attacking Tenerowicz.

Both these places remain open today!

Neither we nor our children can be sure of our life under the conditions at present. While human blood is shed in these gambling houses, public enemies are aiding in conducting the political campaign.

Tenerowicz even came under fire for placing his campaign signs on a building on Conant Avenue across the street from Our Lady Queen of Apostles Church. Whether by coincidence or by design, Tenerowicz's large sign rested between smaller campaign signs for common council candidates Mary Zuk and George Krystalsky, both of whom were reputed to be Communists. For this, Tenerowicz was accused of ridiculing the faith of the people. "How much do these people care for our traditions or religion?" Lewandowski asked.

Maybe they did care, but the voters didn't. Tenerowicz easily won reelection, and shortly thereafter, he was elected to Congress.

In a way, Tenerowicz epitomized Prohibition in Hamtramck. He embodied all of its elements in that he disdained Prohibition with a nod and a wink, reflecting the overwhelming feelings of most Hamtramckans. He paid a price for that, serving a stint in prison, as many Hamtramckans did for breaking the Prohibition laws. Yet through that time, he never lost his touch with the people of Hamtramck. Like a good doctor, he had a splendid bedside manner that extended well beyond the hospital. The people appreciated that and were willing to forgive his sins, either personal or professional.

As for the crime climate of the Tenerowicz years, it might be best summed up by an incident in November 1936 when the common council issued a directive that gambling devices in the city be tracked down and destroyed. "There are hundreds of these 'baffle boards' in Hamtramck and it's about time we got rid of them," said Councilman Joseph Kuberacki. "And I'm not doing this because I lost so much money last night on one machine." He paused and then added, "And I won't say where."

That in itself said something.

And it also helps explain the growing sense of weariness the people were experiencing with the endless parade of charges and indictments, scandals and convictions. And as hard as they might protest, the folks of Hamtramck watched their town cultivate a well-deserved reputation as a lawless town where corruption was tolerated. It wasn't the media to blame for what had happened; it was corrupt politicians and police and a population dominated by complacent and often complicit residents. Tolerating Prohibition was one thing. Gambling, prostitution, bribery and even murder were whole other aspects of a town gone wild.

Then, ever so slowly, change began to occur. Certainly the end of Prohibition had an impact, and the frustration of the people played a role. Perhaps the declining population was a factor. After peaking at fifty-six thousand people in 1930—which was far too many for a town of 2.1

square miles that lacked any tall buildings to house them—Hamtramck's population began a slow but steady decline. This decreased some of the social pressures as demands for services lightened and there simply was more space to breathe. Whatever the reason, going into the 1940s, there was a definite sense that the tide was turning.

There would be a few more murmurs of corruption in the next few years. Mayor Walter Kanar, who would replace Tenerowicz after an internal battle in city hall when Tenerowicz resigned to go on to Congress, would face corruption charges. But they were never prosecuted, and Kanar was not convicted of anything. And with the coming of World War II, the population of Hamtramck was focused in a new direction. Many of the residents had close relatives in Poland, and they watched in horror as Hitler, and later the Soviets, devastated the country. Hamtramck, with the Dodge Main factory at its core, became a major cog in the arsenal of democracy as it shifted from producing cars to war machines. The start of the war also had major social consequences. It ended the Great Depression, and jobs became plentiful. And, of course, the draft was initiated. Suddenly, young men were going into the service and, not long after that, overseas and into combat.

The city was growing up. It was maturing and changing drastically. Prohibition was a memory, and whatever forgiveness there may have been for the blind pigs and brothels evaporated. In 1942, Hamtramck took a major step away from its bawdy past when it elected Dr. Stephen Skrzycki (pronounced Skrit-ski) as mayor. Like Tenerowicz, Skrzycki was a physician and had strong ties to the community. He had previously served on the school board, so he was not a newcomer to politics.

During his ten-year term in office, the political squabbling would be confined to city hall and there would be fewer cases of corruption reported. Not that there weren't issues. The school board became embroiled in a scandal over board members "selling" jobs and accepting bribes to promote employees in 1946. Just a year earlier, the state auditor general had conducted an investigation of dubious expenses incurred by the board. Old habits, it seems, died hard.

And the more familiar forms of vice persisted. A small item carried in the July 28, 1944 edition of the *Citizen* newspaper was typical: "Blind Pig Again Closed by Police." It related that three officers "who chanced upon an alleged blind pig operating Sunday morning while people were on their way to church" closed the place after its operator, Mrs. Salomina Gola, forty-eight, was arrested. Four cases of beer and four cases of whiskey were

Hamtramck's political scene shifted greatly when Dr. Stephen Skrzycki was elected mayor in 1942. His ten-year tenure saw the end of most of the corruption in the city.

confiscated. Six men were found in the building, which was at the rear of a flower shop at 3002 Carpenter Avenue.

There would be more like this, little operations not nearly on the magnitude of the heady days of Prohibition and its immediate aftermath. Vice was no longer a disease in Hamtramck. It was a persistent rash that didn't do great harm but was annoying.

A new element was added with the growth of mutuel betting. This is like the traditional "numbers" racket, which is akin to a lottery with the prize determined by a certain unpredictable but regularly issued number, like the score of a sporting event. It was called "mutuel" because the prize was fixed by the amount of money that was collected in bets and shared among winners. They were extremely popular because they were easy to play and small amounts of money could be bet, much like today's state lotteries.

"There is no widespread gambling in Hamtramck," said Police Chief John J. Wojciszak in February 1947. Wojciszak was being quoted in the *Citizen* newspaper in response to a story that a mutuel operation was uncovered

The Bowery nightclub was a legitimate nightspot that replaced the old speakeasies. Even upstanding citizens would frequent it, including (from left) John Ptaszkiewicz, Arthur Rooks, Bud Benz and Al Strong.

operating out of a candy store on Casmere Street in Hamtramck. "We have nothing to hide," Wojciszak said. "Hamtramck is a clean city." Still, Wojciszak said that mutuel arrests were a near daily occurrence in Hamtramck. He would strengthen that anti-gambling effort by padlocking all buildings where convictions on mutuel operations were handed down by the courts.

In time, even reports of this sort began to fade. Skrzycki's administration was known for its "clean" operations, and the city began to make solid progress in putting its sordid past behind it. It was also during Skrzycki's tenure, in 1943, that the city adopted Civil Service, bringing to an end the corrupting effects of cronyism. The politicians' ability to award lucrative jobs to cronies was severely limited by Civil Service, although that could still be manipulated to a degree.

Hamtramck's population decline also picked up greatly following the end of World War II. This was to be expected. The initial immigrant influx flowed into town, prompting builders to erect houses on narrow lots. There was no need for driveways then because few had cars. Lawns, such as they were, were sparse and often nonexistent. After the war, when the guys began coming home from the service, many were starting new families, and there was almost no place for them to live in the city. Virtually every dwelling was occupied, and conditions were already cramped. People had saved up money during the war years when there were few large items, like cars and refrigerators, to buy as production had been turned over to war manufacturing. With the end of the war, automakers started producing cars again, and people had the money to buy them. The GI Bill also made it possible for almost anyone to get a home mortgage. Finally roads, including some freeways, were being installed, making it even easier for suburb dwellers to commute to the city or more distant factories. New housing development began to spring up in Warren, just north of Detroit. Whole subdivisions were being built, with wide streets, garages, large lots and new infrastructure that promised to keep basements from flooding after hard storms. These were tempting lures.

For Hamtramckans, a natural migration pattern developed, with the earliest émigrés settling at the Outer Drive–Van Dyke section of Detroit, just northeast of the city, then to the city of Warren, about three miles north of Hamtramck and then later to communities like Sterling Heights, Utica, Shelby Township, Troy and others. The city's population plummeted. This wasn't entirely bad. There would be no way Hamtramck could function today with fifty-six thousand residents. Virtually everyone owns cars now; some families have several cars. There simply wouldn't be enough room to accommodate them for parking on the streets. This was less of an issue in the 1940s and 1950s, when most families had only one car, but it still put a strain on the city's infrastructure.

Prosperity, at least to a degree, also came to Hamtramck. It was evolving from a poor immigrant community into a middle-class town. The temptations of the Prohibition and Great Depression years became less alluring. Beer and liquor became plentiful and cheap after Prohibition ended. And it was safe. Illegally made liquor often was brewed or distilled in unsanitary containers, like tubs with lead sealing or even car radiators that were abundant with lead. Some bootleggers even cut the liquor with denatured alcohol or other poisonous substances that could blind or even kill the imbiber. As for the blind pigs and brothels, most closed or moved on to other areas. Tolerance for them grew shorter as young mothers wanted decent neighborhoods in which to raise their kids, whether they were staying in Hamtramck or not.

But some things never end.

"Operators of 'blind pigs' in Hamtramck are being given fair warning by police that they will not tolerate this illicit operation and will halt all practices of this kind that is brought to their attention," the *Citizen* newspaper reported on May 27, 1954. "As a result of closer surveillance, two such places have been raided in the last two weeks. In one raid, a saleswoman was arrested and fined and in the other, the operator and seven loiterers were fined. The second raid made Sunday was at 3400 Goodson, the home of Henry Kaczor, who together with seven 'customers' were taken into custody."

However, even reports like this began to become rare. But while Hamtramckans were cleaning up their act and the town, the thirst for cheap booze remained despite the shrinking market for illegal hooch.

"Federal Men Find Large Still" was the headline in the April 30, 1959 edition of the *Citizen*. And guess where it was? At the old Auto City Brewery, which had closed in 1941. By this point, the building was owned by an ice cream company, which only used a separate part of the building. The owners said they had leased a portion of the building to some folks for $150 a month. The renters said they were going to produce cleaning fluid there, and in fact, the renters gave the owners complimentary bottles of cleaning fluid at Christmas. But they were there to make liquor, 4,300 gallons of which were destroyed by agents from the U.S. Treasury Department's Alcohol and Tobacco Tax Division. Seized were a 270-gallon still; twenty vats of 220-gallon capacity containing mash, which was fermenting; 4,000 pounds of sugar; 1,100 pounds of grain; and more than 500 gallons of liquor, of which 300 was in gallon jugs.

Seven people were arrested for operating the largest still anyone had seen in town in fifteen years. John R. Jones, U.S. assistant attorney, said the still had been in operation for several months. He said it cost about seventy-five cents a gallon to make the moonshine, which was wholesaled at eight dollars. The purchasers would dilute it and sell it for two dollars a pint. Not a bad business model, other than that part about going to jail.

But the size of the operation was unusual. Most moonshiners of this later period were nowhere near that scale. In September 1961, two men, ages twenty and twenty-three, were arrested for operating a still. They were caught when police saw them carrying buckets of moonshine from a house to a barrel by the alley. Police confiscated a 280-gallon cooker, seventeen barrels of mash and other equipment. The men said they were moving the still to a new location when they were caught. Two months later, a twenty-two-year-old man was caught by police when his cooker exploded and set a house on fire on Dubois Street. Police came across the still as they spotted the fire while cruising the neighborhood. Confiscated were a 350-gallon cooker, thirty-two barrels of mash, some corn, sugar, empty jugs and eight jugs filled with moonshine.

And so it went, fairly routinely, in fact. The *Citizen* reported in September 1961, "Ferreting out and destroying illegal whiskey still is becoming a weekly chore for members of the Hamtramck Police department vice squad—detectives Stanley Pudlo, and Emil Niemchak and patrolman Walter Dziurda." That was just after officers had busted up two operations on Dequindre and Dubois Streets. But these were all small operations, nothing like what had been seen in the days of Prohibition.

A few illegal gambling places continued to do business as well. One was housed in the basement of a candy store on Lumpkin Street for many years. The neighborhood kids all knew about it. So did the cops. But eventually it closed, and the building was torn down. However, the ladies of the brothels managed to find a new home. Directly across from the Dodge Main factory on Jos. Campau stood the Berkshire Motel and Robin's Nest Inn. Notorious is a word that hardly does justice to them. Infamous comes closer.

The Berkshire was built in 1965. "It will be modern in design and will contain the latest and most up-to-date motel equipment," the *Citizen* newspaper reported. It had thirty-six units and included the Robin's Nest Lounge. It was designed mainly to cater to Chrysler officials visiting the Dodge Main plant across the street and the many bowlers who came to town to participate in the extremely popular, and lucrative, Citizen Singles Bowling Classic that drew bowlers from across the country. Where it went wrong is not easy to identify. But indeed it did, and quickly. Within a few years, it already had a reputation as a notorious spot. "Sixty-seven arraigned in state's largest prostitution raid ever," the *Citizen* reported on February 5, 1970. The tally included seven prostitutes and sixty persons charged with frequenting a place where "prostitution is practiced and encouraged."

The raid culminated a four-month investigation involving the Wayne County sheriff, who was brought into town at the request of Hamtramck police chief Arthur Chojnacki. "We understand what Chief Chojnacki was up against but it took a long time in a long investigation by the sheriff's officers to work up a case," said Wayne County undersheriff Loren Pittman. "This was done by sending men in the Berkshire, undercover, and watching how this thing operated. The upshot of it all was that on Friday we all felt we had enough information on how it operated to go over to Hamtramck and hit it."

Later in the year, a pair of shootings occurred at the motel, cementing its image as a dangerous spot. In the long term, it didn't matter. In 1979, Chrysler announced it was closing Dodge Main, and a year later, the entire area was vacated as all the structures in the neighborhood were demolished to make way for the new GM Hamtramck-Detroit Assembly plant that was to be constructed there.

Long after Prohibition ended, vice remained in Hamtramck. The Berkshire motel became infamous as a house of prostitution. A major raid was conducted there in 1970.

In a way, the demolition of the Berkshire was the last gasp of the Prohibition era. It was a new building, but its illegal operations were a remnant of Hamtramck's wild days when dozens of speakeasies, brothels and other such businesses thrived in Hamtramck. From this point forward, it would be hard to find any prostitution or bootlegging arrests logged in Hamtramck. From that aspect, the story was over.

But there's more.

CHAPTER 6

TO THE...HANGOVER!

Y ou can't drink for years without feeling the effects when you stop. And
you can't just walk away from your past, although Hamtramck tried
mighty hard to do just that. By the 1950s, when Hamtramck had become
a relatively clean and sober town, the Prohibition and wild years seemed
like the distant past even though most of those who were involved were still
around. But all was forgiven. Almost.

In 1954, City Councilman John Wojtylo raised a firestorm when he
proposed the city eliminate the pensions of certain former city employees
and their widows who were "self-admitted grafters." These included former
policemen Barney Nowicki, William Berg, Joseph Kalinowski and Joseph
Rustoni, among others.

The resolution received no support from the council. In fact, council
president Julia Rooks admonished Wojtylo for picking on widows.
Councilman Henry Kozak went further, ripping into Wojtylo, saying to him,
"You are the most vicious and selfish man I ever knew."

The council may have been mad at Wojtylo just for bringing the
matter up. In fact, a curious development occurred starting in the 1940s
and stretched in the following decades. Like the mobster who goes into
a witness protection program, Hamtramck assumed a new identity. Its
Roaring Twenties persona was replaced by that of hardworking veterans
and churchgoing family folks. No more bombs would be blown up outside
the houses of politicians. The dirtiest trick to be played was subscribing
a rival to *Playboy* magazine without his knowledge so he could look like

Hamtramck and beer are nearly inseparable. They are so close, in fact, that a number of brews have adopted the city's name.

a pervert in the eyes of the mailman and anyone else you might tip off to his supposedly lecherous ways. Or you might suffer the fate of Walter Bednarski, who was running for treasurer in 1940.

Two days before the election, he was arrested and charged with illegally transporting twelve cases of liquor to a bar, which was against the law if you did not have a license to transport liquor. Bednarski could have spent the election behind bars if his friends hadn't rushed to his aid and bailed him out in a matter of hours. What really steamed Bednarski was that this occurred in April 1940. The charges stemmed from an incident that had happened the previous November, when Bednarski was just trying to help a pal move the liquor, which was of the legal variety. What really seemed to be behind the arrest was an attempt to embarrass him just before the election. After all, who was going to elect a guy to be city treasurer as he sat in jail? That would have been a stretch for Hamtramck even in its worst days.

"As far as I'm concerned, it was just another cheap political trick that didn't work," Bednarski said. "The whole thing was phony from beginning to end."

He was right. On May 3, Judge Nicholas Gronkowski ruled that "there is no cause for any further judicial inquiry" and closed the case. Bednarski won the election, but it was never determined who engineered his arrest.

The Nut House was a popular bar that stood (by coincidence) next to the old village hall on Jos. Campau.

But even incidents like that—which really was no more than a dirty trick, although admittedly a pretty good one—became rare. And the bars were still brimming with people. There could never be a stigma attached to booze in Hamtramck, especially when it was legal. You could even take pride in frequenting a place as colorful as the Nut House, a popular watering hold known for its flamboyant character—and characters.

The Bednarski incident was soon forgotten, interred with the scandals of the past. That became the normal mode. But it wasn't as though the folks of Hamtramck just turned their collective back on the past. They buried it. You could find the picture of Mayor Jezewski hanging on the wall in city hall, but ask anyone about him and they would say, "Oh, he was Hamtramck's first mayor. He was a pharmacist." And that was just about it. Ask about speakeasies and who went to prison, and the old-timers would shrug, give a slightly sour look and say, "That's the past."

Only rarely through the years was the sordid history confronted. The *Citizen* editorialized in August 1956 that Hamtramck was an honest town:

> *Yes, Hamtramck has been morally clean for 15 years—due largely to the city's top leadership, the late Mayor S.S. Skrzycki* [he had died in 1954] *and the current chief executive officer, Albert J. Zak. Neither had permitted any organized vice. What did exist was of the hit and run variety, and that was wiped out as fast as it was uncovered. Hamtramck's top leadership today is clean. That cannot be said of all city officials, some of whom have associated themselves with elements which will stop at nothing to return Hamtramck to an open-town status.*

What brought the commentary were local press reports about a scandal in the Downriver community of Ecorse, which oddly has paralleled Hamtramck's woes in a number of ways. Its failings revived, briefly, a mention of Hamtramck's wild days.

Even into the 1970s, attempts to write the history of Hamtramck were discouraged. "There's no need to go there," was a common response. That was understandable, given the way Hamtramckans suffered under the cloak of corruption that tainted the image of the city in the eyes of all of America. People were embarrassed and did not want to do anything that might revive the city's formerly bad image. Old documents were destroyed. Political memorabilia was thrown away. The city retained only the material it legally had to keep or was innocuous, like village assessment rolls. Anything else that was potentially damaging to the city's new image was disposed of.

The intentions were good, but the results were questionable. It's true that no one wanted it brought up that a couple mayors had gone to prison and a couple more had been indicted. And perhaps it's better that the legend of Paddy McGraw be allowed to fade away, especially when it was so hard to justify how the guy who ran one of the biggest whorehouses in the Midwest was also venerated as one of the city's most upstanding citizens.

But what about Maurice Keyworth? He was an educator of legendary proportions. He turned one of the most troubled school districts in America into one of the most respected as the Hamtramck Public School system was recognized as innovative and effective and among the best in the nation. His achievements were shining. Yet his memory was virtually tossed out with the trash because of what others did that had nothing to do with him. If there is a true tragedy in Hamtramck's sorry story of sinfulness, it is in him. He deserved so much more than being forgotten. His untimely death at a young age played a role in his now largely forgotten story, but his legacy was also a victim of the times. Sadly forgotten. Today, there is hardly anyone in Hamtramck who knows who Keyworth Stadium is named for.

That is a bigger shame than all the brothels and spilled beer that ever stained Hamtramck during the Prohibition years and beyond. There were others too. Actors, musicians, scientists, educators and more were relegated to Hamtramck's closed history books. Great things had been achieved in Hamtramck, but no one talked about them. No one preserved the wonderful stories. No one seemed to care.

And it all was for nothing. In fact, it was worse than nothing. Had later Hamtramckans examined the city's past and traced its missteps, they might have avoided at least some of the troubles the city would encounter in later years. Many of the city's failings were identified when they occurred. In 1942, a survey of the city's operations done by the Michigan Municipal League identified a host of problems, such as bad practices, failing leadership and corruption, including "a flagrant use of the spoils system." In real numbers, it showed how the city was spending far more on purchases than other towns and how the notorious pension system adopted in 1938 was bleeding the city. All these factors were plunging Hamtramck into a perpetual financial crisis that would result in financial collapse in the early 1970s and financial problems that persist to this day.

Had the city embraced the report then, it might have taken action to rectify those problems. Instead, there is no indication that anything was done with the document, which ended up as just another chronicle of failure and stowed in the back of a filing cabinet to be forgotten.

Similar examples can be found over and over again in the files that managed to escape destruction. The answers to so many of the city's problems lay in the pages of the past, but nobody wanted to go there. Nobody wanted to accept the truth in the simple reality that Hamtramck is what it is for better and for worse.

Ironically, those who were involved in the shenanigans of those times lost no real standing in the community. Doc Ten was well revered through his life, as was Peter Jezewski. Their sins were forgiven. The same was true for others who were indicted or implicated in the crimes of those times.

In the early 1940s, the Hamtramck Indians social club held an "Old Time Ball" to honor Hamtramck's former village officials. All the surviving early officials were there: John Klinger, Charles Geimer, Dan Minock, Anthony Buhr and more, including Harry Wermuskerken. He was the former police chief who had been sent to prison a scant decade before the Old Time Ball, but he was cited as "a warm-hearted patriot who loves Hamtramck as a brother…We honor and respect him."

Indeed, perhaps Hamtramck was too forgiving of those who looted the city treasury or worked the system to their own ends at the expense of the citizens. Few of them were ever singled out for their deeds. Many, in fact, took what they could from Hamtramck and retired to the suburbs, where they lived off the spoils.

But they, too, are part of the past, and all we can do is accept it. It was not pretty, but it was what happened. Today, there a few reminders of those days.

Step into the bathroom of the New Dodge Bar and you can still see a Prohibition tunnel that once was used to transport liquor into the building.

A Prohibition tunnel remains visible from the bathroom of the New Dodge Bar on Jos. Campau Avenue. It was used to sneak booze into the building from an anonymous building across the alley. There were a number of these tunnels all around town. They provided the bootleggers with a way to move the barrels from inauspicious loading places, like garages, to speakeasies nearby. Perhaps they didn't even need to be so cautious, given the wide-open nature of the town, but it was better to be subdued than brazen.

Paddy McGraw's place is long gone, torn down in 1981 to make way for the General Motors Detroit-Hamtramck Assembly Plant. But there's at least one building on Jos. Campau Avenue that served as a brothel back in the old days that is still standing, although now vacant. And every so often, someone remodeling a house finds an old still tucked away in the basement, attic or even hidden between the walls.

A thriving reminder of that era, however, is shown in the city's bar scene. It isn't anything like it used to be, when there were hundreds of bars packing the town, but there's still a healthy number. But who knows if even they will remain. The majority of Hamtramck's new immigrant population is

The door is at the corner of this building, meaning it likely was a bar in years past. Today, it is a residence.

Muslims from Yemen and Bangladesh. Islam strictly forbids alcohol, and if the political control of the town shifts to a majority of Muslims, they will be less inclined to approve any liquor licenses in the future.

What irony.

But these days, the bars are still serving. They range from tiny shot-and-a-beer places to popular nightclubs that draw a good number of people into town from the suburbs. And many of the old bar buildings that closed long ago have been converted into living spaces. You still see them all over town, as many as two and three at the corners of intersections. You can tell them apart from a nearly equal number of former corner grocery stores by looking at the placement of the door. Generally, if the door is at the corner of the building, it likely was once a saloon. If it is at the center of the building's front, it was a store.

Look and you will find these gentle hints of a not-so-gentle past.

Make of them—and all of this—what you will.

BIBLIOGRAPHY

Blum, Peter H. *Brewed in Detroit*. Detroit: Wayne State University Press, 1999.

Burton, Clarence M. *The City of Detroit, Michigan*. Vol. 2. Detroit: S.J. Clarke Publishing Co., 1922.

Commons, Henry L. "The Town That Hasn't Felt the New Day." *Dearborn Independent*, August 27, 1921.

Detroit Free Press. "Hamtramck Council Recall Threatened." September 26, 1923.

———. "Hamtramck Dives Face Police Drive." September 30, 1923.

———. "Hamtramck May Ask State to Aid Cleanup." September 19, 1923.

———. "Mayor to Stay in Hamtramck." March 26, 1935.

Detroit News. "Graft Jury Names 23 More in Hamtramck." August 21, 1941.

———. "Hamtramck Graft Jury Is Demanded." July 10, 1946.

———. "Survey Flails Hamtramck." January 22, 1942.

———. "Vice, Crime Choke City." June 21, 1928.

Detroit Times. "Book Center of Beer Plot Case." June 29, 1924.

Dunbar, Willis F. Revised by George S. May. *Michigan: A History of the Wolverine State*. Grand Rapids, MI: William B. Eerdmans Publishing Co., 1965.

Financial and Administrative Survey of Hamtramck, Michigan. Ann Arbor: Michigan Municipal League, 1941.

Hamtramck Citizen. "Arrest 5 in Raid on Bling Pig." October 22, 1959.

———. "Blind Pig Again Closed by Police." July 28, 1944.

———. "Blind Pig Is Raided, Six Taken to Court." October 15, 1959.

———. "Blind Pig Operation Is Halted." May 27, 1954.

———. "Chief Denies Return of Vice to Hamtramck." February 7, 1947.

———. "Destroying Whiskey Still Weekly Chore of Police Vice Squad." September 21, 1961.

———. "800 Pay Fines in State Gambling Raids." December 31, 1940.

BIBLIOGRAPHY

————. "Federal Men Find Large Still." April 30, 1959.

————. "Hamtramck Resident Nabbed by Federals." January 17, 1956.

————. "Hamtramck's Naughty Reputation Goes Back to the Roaring Twenties." September 7, 1959.

————. "It's the Tenth Anniversary of Death of Paddy McGraw." June 5, 1946.

————. "McGraw Death Probe Dropped." July 2, 1936.

————. "Paddy McGraw Remembered as a 'Good-Hearted-Guy.'" July 2, 1936.

————. "Sixty-seven Arraigned on State's Largest Prostitution Raid Ever." February 5, 1970.

————. "Wants 'Graft' Widows Off Pension Rolls." October 28, 1954.

————. "Whiskey Making Operations Are Halted by Police Raid." September 14, 1961.

Hamtramck Yearbook, 1947–48.

Holt, Felix C. "The Story of Hamtramck Where Detroiters Cot Their Booze and Night Life Thrills." *Follyology* 1, no. 5 (September 1923): 32–35.

Housing the Children. Hamtramck Public Schools, Board of Education, 1926.

Hyde, Charles, K. *The Dodge Brothers*. Detroit: Wayne State University Press, 2005.

Kavieff, Paul R. *The Violent Years: Prohibition and the Detroit Mobs*. Fort Lee, NJ: Barricade Books, 2001.

Manual, County of Wayne, Michigan 1930. Board of County Auditors, Detroit.

Marsh, Harriet A., and Florence A. Marsh. *History of Detroit for Young People*. Crawfordsville, IN: Lakeside Press, 1935.

New Deal. "Criticize Paper on Vice Attack." December 13, 1935.

————. "Internal Injury Ends Life of Former Saloon Keeper." June 2, 1936.

Orton, Lawrence D. *Polish Detroit and the Kolasinski Affair*. Detroit: Wayne State University Press, 1981.

Palmer, Friend. *The History of Detroit and Michigan*. Detroit: Silas Farmer & Co., 1884.

Plumb, Mildred. *The History of Tau Beta*. Detroit: Evans-Winter-Hebb, Inc., 1938.

The Public School Code of the Hamtramck Public Schools. N.p.: Hamtramck Board of Education, 1927.

Radzilowski, Thaddeus C. "The Polish Experience in Detroit." Paper, St. Mary's College of Ave Maria University, Orchard Lake, 2001.

————. *St. Florian Parish, 75 Years*. Detroit: St. Florian, 1983.

Rubenstein, Nathan D. "The Ghosts of Pleasures Past." Detroit News Magazine, March 22, 1981.

Saginaw News Courier. "Hamtramck Mayor Called Insincere." February 1, 1924.

————. "State Will Send Additional Men." February 1, 1924.

Smith, Bruce. *The State Police*. New York: McMillan Co., 1925.

Social Pioneer. "The Story of the Tau Beta Association." Detroit, 1926.

Time. "Miscellany." September 27, 1943.

Washington Times. "5-Cent Bread Firm Blown Up by Rivals in Detroit." January 26, 1922.

Woods, Arthur Evans. *Hamtramck, Then and Now*. New York: Bookman Associates Books, 1955.

INDEX

ABOUT THE AUTHOR

Greg Kowalski has been in communications for nearly forty years. During that time, he served as editor of several newspapers, including the *Hamtramck Citizen*, *Birmingham Eccentric*, *West Bloomfield Eccentric* and *Southfield Eccentric*. In addition, he has written eight local history books, including six on Hamtramck. He also has written for and edited numerous books, magazines, newsletters and related material, including writing articles for *Michigan History* magazine. He also has done corporate communications and public relations.

A lifelong resident of Hamtramck, he has been the chairman of the Hamtramck Historical Commission since it was founded in 1998. He and the other members of the commission have worked for fifteen years to establish the new Hamtramck Historical Museum, which opened in 2013.

He is a member of several historical societies, including serving on the board of Preservation Bloomfield, and is a member of the Algonquin Club (historical society), the Michigan Historical Society and the Oakland County Pioneer and Historical Society. He is a former member of the Wayne State University College of Fine, Professional and Communication Arts Alumni board of directors.

Visit us at
www.historypress.net
....
This title is also available as an e-book